There is one way of overcoming our
ghostly enemies: spiritual mirth and a
perpetual bearing of God in our minds.

S t .   A n t h o n y

This is what the LORD says, he who made the earth,
the LORD who formed it and established it—
the LORD is his name: "Call to me
and I will answer you and tell you great
and unsearchable things you do not know."

J e r e m i a h   3 3 : 2 - 3

WHY DON'T I GET WHAT I PRAY FOR?

John W. Cowart

INTERVARSITY PRESS
DOWNERS GROVE, ILLINOIS 60515

For Gin

I prayed twenty-five years ago
to get over loving you.
I'm so glad that God
did not answer my prayer.

InterVarsity Press® is the book-publishing division of InterVarsity Christian Fellowship®, a student movement active on campus at hundreds of universities, colleges and schools of nursing in the United States of America, and a member movement of the International Fellowship of Evangelical Students. For information about local and regional activities, write Public Relations Dept., InterVarsity Christian Fellowship, 6400 Schroeder Rd., P.O. Box 7895, Madison, WI 53707-7895.

Cover photograph: Robert Flesher

ISBN 0-8308-1344-6

Printed in the United States of America ♾

Library of Congress Cataloging-in-Publication Data
Cowart, John W.
    Why don't I get what I pray for? / John W. Cowart.
        p.   cm.
    ISBN 0-8308-1344-6
    1. Prayer—Christianity.   I. Title.
BV220.C683   1993   *93-3527*
248.3'2—dc20   *CIP*

| 15 | 14 | 13 | 12 | 11 | 10 | 9 | 8 | 7 | 6 | 5 | 4 | 3 | 2 | 1 |
| 04 | 03 | 02 | 01 | 00 | 99 | 98 | 97 | 96 | 95 | 94 | 93 |

Introduction
Why Don't I Get What I Pray For?

If a fisherman who believes God answers prayer goes fishing early one morning and prays really hard all day to catch a fish, but does not even get a nibble, what does that mean?

Once, while interviewing some children for a newspaper article on kids' views of God, I posed this question to the group. The question did not faze the seven-year-old theologians. "It's because the fish prayed harder," answered one little girl blithely.

Even children know some prayer "works" immediately and some doesn't.

One Saturday morning recently, my son Donald, who is seventeen, prayed for a new computer. Within two hours, Tim Temple, a computer programmer we hardly knew at the time, came to our door with several big boxes filled with computer, monitor, printer, mouse and loads of software—a gift for Donald!

That same morning, I once again had prayed for something I've been praying for every day over the past thirteen years—zilch.

I have prayed for scads of things without hearing so much as a whisper from heaven. I am the World's Foremost Authority on Unanswered Prayer.

Oddly enough, other Christians contend for my title; it seems that many—are you among them?—pray for things they don't get.

Why, when a prayer is answered, it's so unusual that we stand up in church and testify!

Jets and Sailing Ships

Sometimes I wish I could think about prayer in terms of moving from point A to points B, C, D and E in logical order to arrive at a neat conclusion. In that case, I could write a book called *Five Easy Steps for Getting Prayers Answered.*

But prayer does not work that way for me.

When I think one of my prayers is not answered, I hurt. The lack of an answer confuses me. I feel lost and bewildered. I get scared. I want spiritual things to go from point A to point E, easy as one, two, three, but they don't. Sometimes prayer seems to be a journey through strange and frightening terrain rather than an arrival. But, taken as a whole, the journey resembles a vacation excursion with fun, laughter, interesting companions, beautiful vistas and shady rest stops more than it resembles trudging through a desert. Here's what I mean.

On TV during Desert Storm, I saw jet pilots fly five hundred miles to a particular place and practically knock on the front door of a specific building . . .

Knock. Knock.

Who's there?

Ka.

Ka who?

Ka-boom!

About the time the war was going on, I was reading the diary of Christopher Columbus. In those pages I saw that the admiral pointed his ship toward where he thought land might be and then blundered all over the ocean till he arrived at a destination.

I noticed that both the jet pilot and the sailing-ship captain did eventually get where they needed to be.

In my thinking I'm much closer to the old-time sailor than to the jet pilot, so please bear with me if my book seems at times to drift off course when it comes to prayer. I nose into backwaters and investigate tiny inlets, and sometimes I do get stuck on sandbars that more logical, hi-tech Christians may sail right on past—but I often see footprints on those sandbars. I'm not the first Christian to run aground here. And still others who follow may get stuck in these odd places too, so I hope this book will act as a shoal marker if nothing else.

Questioning from Pain

Thinking about the question "Why doesn't God answer my prayer?" is not an idle intellectual exercise. The people I've heard ask this question have been people in pain, people who were confused, people who even felt betrayed by God, people who find that they can't live by bumper-sticker slogans promising easy answers. People who have felt just like I have.

As I write this book, I'm aware of the pain raised by the questions I examine. And I'm aware that I have no easy answers to present. I'm no jet pilot; I don't think my book will get you to a specific door in a particular building with a spiritual bang. But I hope that by thinking through the question of unanswered prayers together, you and I will at least sail within sight of land—and from there we'll see a lighthouse and even find a safe harbor.

Many Christians question why prayer only sometimes works as we expect it to. Is something wrong with my faith, my sins, my breath? This book will consider such questions. We will look at unanswered prayer from three interwoven perspectives: biblical, historical and personal.

The book will discuss a number of issues: Is anybody out there to hear our prayers? Where is God when I want him? Is God too weak to perform what I ask? Does God care enough to answer? What sin have I committed that makes him too mad to answer?

Of course the big question is "Has Cowart bit off more than he can chew in addressing such a deep subject?"

Maybe so; after all, I have been praying about this book for a long time.

We Are Not Alone

Ancient tradition says that the apostle John prayed so much that calluses grew on his knees. My name is John, and I'm a Christian too, but no calluses grow on my knees. My calluses are elsewhere; as a professional writer, I sit and type a lot, so naturally my calluses are on my fingers.

But I do pray.

Sometimes I pray silently, sometimes out loud, off the top of my head.

Sometimes I read my prayers from a book. Sometimes I pray continuously for hours on end. Usually I lead my family in prayer after supper each night—unless there's something good on TV. Occasionally I enjoy a private devotional quiet time every single day—till the mood leaves me. Every once in a while I get peeved at God and refuse to pray at all for weeks at a time.

Am I the only Christian in town who follows such an erratic pattern of prayer? Or am I typical?

Occasionally I do get exactly what I pray for. Most of the time I don't.

Why not?

That question bothers me. It has bothered many other Christians I've known too.

Madge prayed to keep her breast. She lost it to cancer.

Joan prayed for her son to live. He died.

Bill and Petula prayed to become overseas missionaries; every mission board they applied to turned down their application.

St. Paul prayed for God to remove his thorn in the flesh; it stayed.

Tina prayed for Dick to marry her. At the same time, Dick was praying about marrying Jean, and Jean was praying for Martin to marry her. Nobody in that little Christian prayer circle got what they prayed for!

Every one of these Christians was a decent, upright person. Every one of their prayers was for something good, wholesome and honorable. None of their prayers seems at odds with Holy Scripture.

In some of these cases, two or three of us did agree to make the request in Jesus' name, and we did ask for God's will to be done. Yet we did not get the specific thing we asked God for. It seems as though we should have.

Jesus Makes Promises

The promises of Jesus are sweeping in scope when it comes to prayer. Here's one from each Gospel:

When you pray, go into your room, close the door and pray to your Father, who is unseen. Then your Father, who sees what is done in secret, will reward you. (Matthew 6:6)

Therefore I tell you, whatever you ask for in prayer, believe that you have received it, and it will be yours. (Mark 11:24)

So I say to you: Ask and it will be given to you; seek and you will find; knock and the door will be opened to you. For everyone who asks receives; he who seeks finds; and to him who knocks, the door will be opened. (Luke 11:9)

And I will do whatever you ask in my name, so that the Son may bring glory to the Father. You may ask me for anything in my name, and I will do it. (John 14:13-14)

Yes, I do know that reading each full passage for loopholes reveals certain conditions for answered prayer. We'll examine these and other sections of Scripture in future chapters. But at first reading, it looks to me as though Jesus makes some comprehensive promises concerning prayer. It looks as though he says over and over again in Scripture that he will give us the things we ask for in prayer.

Yet again and again, I have asked without receiving what I asked for.

"Spiritual" Prayers

I have been told that prayer is a sweet mystical union with God, that in the presence of his awesome majesty human lips are silenced, that the soul can be so overcome with worship that we ask nothing other than God himself. I've been told that the purpose of mature prayer is to bask in God's presence, asking nothing, and that to pray for "things" is to pray on a childish, primitive level.

Maybe so.

But I agree with poet John Tyler Pettee, who wrote:

Pray of peace and grace and spiritual food,

For wisdom and guidance,

For all these are good,

But don't forget the potatoes.

It seems to me that people who expound an ethereal view of prayer fall into one of four categories:

(1) Deeply spiritual saints who are caught up in the love of God. Such a one was Archbishop François Fénelon, who served Christ in the notoriously corrupt French court of King Louis XIV. He prayed:

Lord, I know not what I ought to ask of Thee. Thou only knowest what we need; Thou lovest me better than I know how to love myself. O Father, give to Thy child that which he himself knows not how to ask. I dare not ask either for crosses or consolations; I simply present myself before Thee, I open my heart to Thee. Behold my needs which I know not myself; see and do according to Thy tender mercy. Smite, or heal; depress me, or raise me up; I adore all Thy purposes without knowing them; I am silent; I offer myself in sacrifice; I yield myself to Thee; I would have no other desire than to accomplish Thy will. Teach me to pray; pray Thyself in me—Amen.

(2) Affluent Christian materialists who have already made their pile and risen beyond the mundane concerns that I have, such as flat tires and no spare, late bills or frustrating jobs.

(3) Religious worldlings who don't believe that God answers prayer anyhow, so they don't bother to ask. Asking God for stuff is a waste of breath because they know they're not going to get it, but they do like to go through the motions of prayer.

(4) Everyday Christians who have experienced unanswered prayers and have just about given up on prayer but feel uncomfortably guilty and wish their prayers were real and effective. But they aren't; so they settle for a "spiritual" interpretation of prayer.

Materialistic Prayers

Now, I am also aware that some unscrupulous people make merchandise of the idea of material answers to prayer. They preach a gospel of materialistic prosperity in which God is supposed to load down petitioners with homes, cars, boats, jewels and gold watches. If you mail them your seed money, they'll let you in on the secret to their seedy prayers. What an abomination!

The God of the Bible is likely to give us just as many gold watches as Jesus wore. Jesus is our Master; we are his servants. Can servants expect to live better than their master?

I reject the idea that God gives goodies for the sake of goodies, and also the idea that he gives only warm fuzzy feelings when we pray.

The God and Father of our Lord Jesus Christ is just that: God and Father. In our conversations with him he treats us within the framework of those two relationships. And after all, God is the one who initiates prayer in the first place. "The Spirit helps us in our weakness. We do not know what we ought to pray for, but the Spirit himself intercedes for us with groans that words cannot express" (Romans 8:26).

So, I suppose, it may be logical to think about possible causes for unanswered prayers first as they may relate to God's nature, then as they may relate to our own nature. Anyhow, that's my general plan for approaching the subject of unanswered prayers in this book.

You'll find that from time to time I quote from other authors. If you are interested in tracking down any of these quotations, please refer to the bibliography at the end of the book, which lists my sources alphabetically by author.

— one —

Is Anybody Out There?

If there is no God

to answer prayers, then obviously

I will get no answers.

PICTURE SOMETHING RIDICULOUS WITH ME. IMAGINE THAT prayer is a telephone—as in that old camp meeting song "Jesus Is on the Line, Tell Him What You Want."

Imagine dialing D-E-A-R G-O-D and hearing four rings. Then a peppy voice answers: "Hi. This is God. I can't come to the phone right now, but if you will leave your name, number and a brief message—no more than thirty seconds, please—after the tone, I will get back to you as soon as I can. Have a nice day. BEEP!"

That never happens. God does not use an answering machine. In fact, I'm sure that heaven is one place you'll never find answering machines at all.

Neither does a bored receptionist screen God's calls to keep the riffraff from bothering him. When we call upon the name of the Lord, not even the archangel Gabriel answers; God himself hears our call and listens.

Or does he?

Am I Talking to Myself?

At a meeting I attended, Steve prayed to be able to make an evangelistic trip to Alaska. At the same meeting, I prayed for money enough to pay our light and water bills.

At the next week's meeting, Steve testified that a Christian businessman had given him a brand-new, straight-off-the-show-room-floor, fully equipped camper van and money enough to make his trip to Alaska.

Hallelujah! Praise God!

But I did not testify at that second meeting. The local power authority had cut our lights and water off. They stayed off for ten long weeks, till I had earned enough to pay the overdue bills.

When I called on God, I received no immediate answer. I did not get his answering machine. I didn't even hear static on the line.

That sometimes makes me worry that the phone is ringing in an empty house. Could it be that no one is there to take my call?

Is there even really a God out there for me?

Are vivid answers to prayer, such as Donald's getting his computer and Steve's getting his van, just matters of coincidence that would have happened anyhow whether anyone prayed or not?

Super Christians with strong faith may not ask such questions. Simple Christians who rest in childlike faith may not question either. But most of us fall somewhere in the middle, and while we seldom voice such doubts in church, we wonder if God is really out there when we get no answer to our prayers.

When God Flunked My Test

I have a long history of doubt when it comes to prayer. Before I became a Christian thirty years ago, I dabbled in Westernized Eastern religions and called myself an agnostic leaning toward atheism. When a missionary witnessed to me about Christ and I began to feel convicted over my personal sinfulness, I came up with a clever plan to use prayer to test God. I prayed, "Okay God, if you're out there, then make such-and-such happen by noon tomorrow. If that happens, then—well, I'll examine you more closely; but if it does not happen, then I'll know for sure that there is no God." Such-and-such did not happen. God flunked my test.

But I'm a generous guy; I wanted to give poor God every chance. I tried the same prayer-test again and again.

I held out the hoop, but he would not jump through it.

Sometimes God can be very uncooperative. He will not be manipulated. He will not be controlled by us. He was not on trial. I was.

When we pray, we do not negotiate a contract between equals. God is Creator, we are creatures. We have no rights we can demand, except for those he chooses to grant us.

Yearning

Anyhow, although God would not perform when I commanded him to, the more I prayed and pestered him, the more I felt—well, the only word I can think of is *hungry*. More and more hungry for God. It got to the point where I wanted him whether he was there to pass my childish tests or not.

He gave me a sense of longing, of yearning, of thirsting. This intense desire that I felt contained an element of incredible sweetness, a heart-pain I loved to feel.

My mind protested, "John, it's crazy to want something that does not exist."

Exactly!

All humans feel thirsty and want water. Naturally. There is such a thing as water.

All of us feel hunger and want food. Naturally. There is such a thing as food.

We feel lust. Naturally. There is such a thing as sex.

Every person sometimes feels a heart-longing for the Eternal. Naturally . . . There is such a thing as God.

We don't want what ain't; we want what is. And God is. He is as real as water, food, sex or anything else you really want. In his *Confessions,* the great theologian St. Augustine speaks of a God-shaped niche in the human soul where nothing less than God fits. I picture this niche as a vacuum inside us, like a black hole in space, which can be filled to capacity by the Infinite but which sucks in everything else and still remains empty. A vacuum demands filling.

Even when we are little kids we feel this emptiness of soul and we hunger to fill it. I remember lying awake at night on the sofa and thinking about God, big and huge (in my five-year-old mind there was a distinction) and sweet, so sweet as to be hugged and hugged and hugged; yet scary too, the awesomeness of the Creator that is totally foreign to all created things.

When I tried to describe my sleepless feelings to my mother, she thought I was trying to talk about Billie Michelle, the little girl who lived next door.

"Puppy love," Mama said. "Isn't that cute? Johnny's got puppy love."

Grrrr! How do you write a five-year-old boy's snarl? No way did I love Billie Michelle. She was a *girl,* for heaven's sakes. If the gnawing hunger meant puppy love, then who needed it?

I think this same dynamic works again and again in everyone's life. When we were young and sought the meaning of existence, the world, the flesh and the devil dismissed our yearning as adolescent growing pains. We hungered for eternity, and they said it was just hormones flowing. The worldly-wise voices teased that we were only hungry for sex. "You need a woman; you need a man," they said.

To a young adult the wise voices whisper, "You hunger for success. Advance in the company. Get trappings: Lear jet, board membership, Gold Card. Success is what you want."

As we mature, the voices of the world, the flesh and the devil say, "What you are hungry for is security. Buy bonds. Get a home. An insurance policy is what you need. Security is what will make the hunger pangs go away."

But the deep hunger of the soul never ceases.

When we sprout white hair, yet still know that heart-longing ache for Something, or Someone, the devil taunts, "You silly old fool! You're just longing for your lost youth."

Thus many of us are tricked into never getting the one thing we want most desperately. And we die just as we lived—desiring the Eternal but settling for mere glitter.

But There Is Hope

King David—the slayer of giant Goliath, the sweet psalmist of Israel, a man of wealth, power and position, a man who possessed all this world had to offer—understood the heart-hunger that you and I experience.

O God, you are my God,
    earnestly I seek you;
my soul thirsts for you,
    my body longs for you
in a dry and weary land
    where there is no water. (Psalm 63:1)

David takes up this theme again and again:

As the deer pants for streams of water,
    so my soul pants for you, 0 God.
My soul thirsts for God, for the living God. (Psalm 42:1)
You open Your hand
    And satisfy the desire of every living thing. . . .
He will fulfill the desire of those who fear Him.
      (Psalm 145:16, 19 NKJV)

If even this king panted, hungered and thirsted, if he longed and desired and yearned for God, then surely the whole thing is much too complex for those of us who merely feel vague whims toward an undefined "something better" now and then.

Not so. We tend to make godly living into a complex mare's nest of worry. That is not the way it works. King David teaches us how to focus and find joy in a way that's simple yet profound. He said, "Trust in the LORD and do good; dwell in the land and enjoy safe pasture. Delight yourself in the LORD and he will give you the desires of your heart" (Psalm 37:3).

Trust and do.

Then you can dwell, enjoy, be safe, delight—and God will give you the desire of your heart.

Think of that! The desire of your heart. The single thing you've hungered for most all of your life is right at your fingertips. How wonderful. How utterly wonderful!

Now, while every person knows that deep, secret desire, we should be cautious about building an esoteric theology on yearning. The universal yearning of humankind for God is just one hint that there is Someone out there somewhere to hear our prayers. There are other hints. In the next chapter, let's look at that yearning some more, along with two other hints of God's presence.

two

Mules, Oxen
and Skunks

If God exists

but he's not available when we pray,

then I get no answers.

THE GREEK PHILOSOPHER SOCRATES USED A MULE TO ARGUE FOR the existence of God. It didn't work. His enemies executed him anyhow. Made him drink poison hemlock.

The Hebrew prophet Isaiah used an ox and an ass in his reasoning about God's existence. He got executed too. They sawed him in half.

Me? As a Christian, I like to play it safe; when I talk about God's existence, I use a skunk for my argument. That makes me smarter than Socrates. At least nobody thinks I'm worth executing. Maybe it's just that nobody wants to talk theology with a skunk.

The First Cause

When Socrates was on trial for his life in Athens, he pointed to a mule plodding past the Theater of Dionysus, where the trial was being held. He observed that mules never produce baby mules. All mules are sterile. Mules are the offspring of female horses mated with male donkeys.

Therefore, the philosopher argued, every time you see a mule, that proves the existence of at least one horse and one donkey. And since all life springs only from other life, the horse and the donkey must have parents too. Then the parents must have parents, and so on and on till you come to an original source of life—God.

Following the law of cause and effect, when you see any effect, you know it must have a cause, and the First Cause of all effects is God, Socrates reasoned.

"Who in the world would believe in sons of gods if they did not believe in gods?" Socrates asked. "That would be just as odd as believing in sons of horses or asses, but not in the horses or asses themselves!"

His enemies responded to his reasoning with a sophisticated argument of their own. "Here, drink this," they said.

The Ox Knows the Way Home

The prophet Isaiah also used an animal analogy to reason with people about God: "The ox knows his master, the donkey his owner's manger, but Israel does not know, my people do not understand" (Isaiah 1:3).

Walt Disney movies and *Reader's Digest* magazine both understand the validity of Isaiah's observation. Every once in a while, one or the other portrays the story of some family going on vacation with their dog or cat. Somehow the animal gets left behind and makes its way over a thousand miles of rough terrain to arrive home. A joyous reunion follows. Everybody hugs everybody. Tears flow.

The story, whatever the animal or the details, touches our hearts. Deep down, we know exactly what the story teaches, and with full hearts we rejoice.

If dumb animals hunger for home and know how to get there,

then why don't people recognize God, who is our Home?

Fact is, we do. We just hate to admit it.

A deep hunger and longing in the human heart manifests itself as a yearning for something. We crave something, and we do know what it is; we know that what we desperately seek is not something, but Someone.

We know this, but sin keeps us from the desire of our hearts, the Desire of all nations—God. And we pretend that we are dumber than Isaiah's ox, that we don't really know.

Isaiah also addresses this false thinking:

> "Come now, let us reason together,"
> says the LORD.
> "Though your sins are like scarlet,
> they shall be as white as snow;
> though they are red as crimson,
> they shall be like wool." (Isaiah 1:18)

In other words, God's message is *come home.*

Jesus said that in the Father's house many mansions—not just buildings but homes—are being prepared for us. Jesus' message is always "Welcome home, stranger!"

Even Skunks Believe

So Socrates' mule argues for God's being the First Cause of all effects. Isaiah's ox argues for God's being the answer to the yearning of our hearts. What does Cowart's skunk argue for?

Years ago, when I lived in Maryland, I used to hike in the Patuxent Wildlife Refuge, a bird sanctuary where huge flocks of ducks gathered in marsh ponds during their migrations. A park ranger there once explained to me that something was killing the baby ducks. He said that overzealous hunters had blasted most of the area's skunks. Because a favorite food of the skunks was snapping-turtle eggs, now the ponds were overrun with snapping turtles, and the favorite food of the turtles was duckling.

Skunks are vital to the food chain! No skunks, no ducks. Nothing left but hungry snapping turtles.

Skunks prove there is an order to creation. The whole scheme of things fits together. It's all balanced. You could almost say it was planned.

A plan means a Planner. A design demands a Designer. A creation requires a Creator.

Theologians say that Socrates' mule illustrates an ontological argument for God's existence; Isaiah's ox illustrates an argument from humans' universal desire for God; and Cowart's skunk illustrates a teleological argument.

For centuries, some very smart people have discussed many arguments and counterarguments concerning the existence of God. If you want more information on the subject, I'd suggest that you read books by heavy-hitter theologians such as St. Augustine, John Calvin, Charles Hodge, Søren Kierkegaard, C. S. Lewis or A. W. Tozer.

The thoughts I've presented here do not necessarily prove the existence of a God who hears and answers our prayers. These thoughts are merely hints that he really is at home when the phone rings. And you don't have to be a super-brain theologian to take a hint.

As St. Paul said, "Anyone who comes to him must believe that he exists and that he rewards those who earnestly seek him" (Hebrews 11:6).

Okay. I believe that God is. I believe he is a rewarder. I even believe that I've been more or less diligent in my prayers. How come I still get no satisfactory answer?

Where is God when I cry for him? Could it be that God is not available?

Where Is God?

According to an old book on odd wills, many years ago an eccentric woman who lived in Cherokee County, North Carolina, died and left her property to God.

The probate court, attempting to honor her wishes, went through the motions of summoning God to court for the settlement. He did not appear.

Pursuing both letter and spirit of the law, the court instructed the local sheriff to locate the designated heir. After a time the sheriff duly reported, "Having searched diligently, I have determined that you cannot find God in Cherokee County, North Carolina."

Where would you find him then?

A missionary on leave from service in India told me that he had seen a man go from boulder to boulder in the desert, knocking on each rock and calling out, "Are you there? Are you there?"

When asked, the man explained he had heard that a god lived among the rocks, and he was looking so he could worship it.

Once I talked with a young woman who was pushing a baby stroller. In it rested a severely deformed and retarded child.

"Where was God when he was born?" she asked bitterly, pointing at her son.

Where is God?

Read any newspaper and you'll find the devil right there in big print on the front page; but where is God?

A basic tenet of Christian theology is that God is omnipresent—that he is everywhere, in all places at all times, unlimited by distance. "In him we live and move and have our being," St. Paul told the philosophers of Athens (Acts 17:28).

The picture the Scripture gives of God's omnipresence reminds me of a piping-hot, batter-fried shrimp. The shrimp is me. The covering batter is the world around me. The oil coating the whole is the extended universe.

And God?

Well, God is the heat that fills and permeates the whole thing—

the shrimp, the batter and the oil.

The Bible teaches that God is in nature—or more correctly, that nature is in God:

The earth is the LORD's, and everything in it,
    the world, and all who live in it. (Psalm 24:1)

The Bible teaches that God is in Christ, his Son: "God was in Christ reconciling the world to Himself" (2 Corinthians 5:19 NKJV).

The Bible teaches that God is in his people, the church. Jesus said, "For where two or three come together in my name, there am I with them" (Matthew 18:20).

The Bible teaches that God is willing to come into the hearts of sinners who repent, folks like you and me: "Here I am! I stand at the door and knock. If anyone hears my voice and opens the door, I will come in and eat with him" (Revelation 3:20).

The Bible teaches that God delights to be discovered by those who truly seek him. As the old hymn (based on Isaiah 44:3) says,

I will pour water on him who is thirsty.

I will pour floods upon the dry ground.

Open your hearts to the gift I am bringing;
    while ye are seeking me, I will be found.

Where is God?

French mystic Jeanne Guyon said the Spirit told her, "While you were running around, I was seeking you."

How about that?

God is near.

Close.

Close as thought. Close as prayer. Close as your heart's desire.

In him we live and move and have our very being.

All Times and Places

God is omnipresent; he is in all places at all times. He is in your kitchen, your office, your garage, your classroom as well as your church. He is with us when we drive, when we polish our shoes, study our lessons, witness to the unsaved, rock the baby, kneel for Communion, feed the hungry, nurse the sick, play ball with the guys . . .

Where is he not?

As you think about God being everywhere watching you, please don't get the mental picture of Big Brother spying on you all the time, ready to zap you when you screw up. Instead, think of a nurse in a hospital intensive-care unit, ready to jump to your aid the second the heart monitor fluctuates.

Jeremy Taylor, who suffered persecution by Oliver Cromwell's Roundheads, said:

God is everywhere present by His power. He rolls the orbs of heaven with His hand; He fixes the earth with His foot; He guides all the creatures with His eye, and refreshes them with His influence; He makes the powers of hell to shake with His terrors, and binds the devils with His word, and throws them out with His command; and sends the angels on embassies with His decrees; He hardens the joints of infants, and makes firm the bones when they are fashioned secretly. . . .

Let everything you see represent to your spirit the presence, the excellency and the power of God, and let your conversation with the creatures lead you unto the Creator; for so shall your actions be done more frequently with an actual eye to God's presence by your often seeing Him in the glass of the creation. In the face of the sun you may see God's beauty; in the fire you may feel His heat warming; in the water His gentleness to refresh you; He it is that comforts your spirit when you have taken cordials; it is the dew of heaven that makes your field give you bread.

Taylor said that if we will but recognize that we live each moment in the presence of God, we can pray anytime and anywhere so that "every act of complaint or thanksgiving, every act of rejoicing or of mourning, and every petition is a going to God, an appearing in

His presence, and a building to God of a chapel in our heart. It reconciles Martha's employment with Mary's devotion, charity and religion, the necessities of our calling and the employment of devotion. For thus, in the midst of the works of your trade, you may retire into your chapel, your heart—and converse with God!"

Trust and do.

God is really beside us constantly, and we can talk with him as we do our everyday work—we can pray without ceasing.

Poet Gerard Manley Hopkins wrote, "To lift up the hands in prayer gives God glory, but a man with a dungfork in his hand, a woman with a slop-pail, give him glory too. He is so great that all things give him glory if you mean they should."

So we don't have to go to a special place; we can pray while we vacuum the floor, program the computer, paint the eaves, change a tire, change the printer ribbon, change the baby.

Work and Prayer

Work is prayer in that by both activities we seek to bring about a desired end. I suspect that the most effective way to work is to pray at the same time, and the most effective way to pray is while our hands are busy with some needed chore.

If in a Chinese restaurant you can eat two bowls of shrimp egg foo young with two chopsticks, how many bowls can you eat with one chopstick? I think work and prayer are like those two chopsticks. We should use both at the same time.

But is this idea for everyone? Yes. While few of us can build a great cathedral, go as missionaries, preach to thousands or perform some great work for God, all of us can do little everyday things for the love of God.

In *The Practice of the Presence of God,* Brother Lawrence, who worked in a monastery kitchen during the 1660s, said that God does not regard the greatness of our labor as much as he regards the love with which it is performed. He tried to cook meals and wash dishes for the love of Christ, and he talked with Christ as he scrubbed pans. He said his greatest busyness did not divert him from the presence of God, because he prayed as he worked.

"The time of business does not with me differ from the time of prayer," he said. "In the noise and clatter of my kitchen, while several persons are at the same time calling for different things, I possess God in as great tranquillity as if I were upon my knees at the blessed sacrament."

Taylor and Lawrence and many other saints of the past say that praying while doing the plain, ordinary, unglamorous duty that is right before our eyes is the best way to pray. They teach that when our prayers seem to get nowhere, we should not sulk but do the obvious duty we have to do. Clean your room. Study your lessons. Witness to the unsaved. Pet the cat. Visit a shut-in. Hoe weeds—praying all the while.

But if God is indeed everywhere and we can talk with him at any time and in any place even while we're doing other things, why do we have any problem at all finding him?

Who's Looking for Whom?
The trouble with an omnipresent God is that he's too close. He crowds us. He moves in on our turf—"Hey, I'm the king of this corner." There are times when we all wish he'd back off, go hide under that rock in India, stop meddling in our affairs.

We become aware of his presence at the most inconvenient times. Yes indeed, sometimes God is not only here and there, but right underfoot.

You see, while we dabble at searching for God and go through all the right religious motions, God is everywhere and at all times seeking us.

Remember, after the first sin of humankind, the very first thing God said was, "Adam, where are you?" Adam, of course, was hiding stark naked in the bushes (Genesis 3:8-10).

That's where we spend most of our time to this very day. Sin causes us to feel an aversion to God, makes us uncomfortable in his presence.

Adam set the historical precedent of God's looking for human-kind while humanity hides. Yet we make a big display of being "seekers" after God. "Where is God? Where is God?" we cry, as though he were the one hiding.

Where is God when the drugs I took deform my child? Where is God when the car breaks down? Where is God when the rent comes due? Where is God when I get fired from my job?

Where is God at those times when I command his appearance front-and-center at my convenience? He really ought to jump when I snap. What kind of God is this, anyway?

He is Creator, and the universe he created, small as a hazelnut, exists in the palm of his hand. He is its Maker, Master and Means of support.

Why Does God Seek Us?

What is it that God wants from me?

Why does he call us to prayer and fellowship?

Why does he call our names and seek out our hiding places?

Why does he beat the bushes for us?

The Bible tells why: "For the eyes of the LORD run to and fro throughout the whole earth, *to show Himself strong on behalf of those whose heart is loyal to Him*" (2 Chronicles 16:9 NKJV).

Amazing!

But if God is strong and he wants to show his strength for me when I pray, but I still do not get the things I ask him for, could it be that God is not strong *enough* to perform? Could it be that he is not *able* to do what I ask?

Let's think about that disturbing possibility in the next chapter.

— three —

Does God Have
the Clout to Do
What We Ask?

If God is able to answer, then why doesn't he?

REMEMBER THE STORY OF DANIEL IN THE LIONS' DEN? Political enemies, observing that Daniel prayed three times daily, engineered a trap, tricking King Darius into making such prayer illegal. Darius liked Daniel and was distressed at being forced to feed him to the lions. While Daniel was in the pit, the king spent a sleepless night.

At the first light of dawn, the king got up and hurried to the lions' den. When he came near the den, he called to Daniel in an anguished voice, "Daniel, servant of the Living God, has your God, whom you serve continually, been able to rescue you from the lions?"

Daniel answered, "O king, live forever! My God sent his angel, and he shut the mouths of the lions. They have not hurt me."

The king, filled with joy, ordered that Daniel be lifted out of the den; he then threw Daniel's enemies in. "And before they reached the floor of the den, the lions overpowered them and crushed all their bones" (Daniel 6:1-24).

Now "Daniel in the Lions' Den" is a neat little Sunday-school story for kids, but the question King Darius asked is one that has been asked over and over again for generations.

"Is God able to ____ ____ ____?" You fill in the blanks.

If God is able, then why doesn't he?

Smashing Cinder Blocks

David the giant-killer said, "Praise be to the LORD my Rock, who trains my hands for war, my fingers for battle. He is my loving God and my fortress, my stronghold and my deliverer" (Psalm 144:1-2).

I get a kick out of that verse, because it reminds me of how twenty-five years and fifty pounds ago I was able break cinder blocks with my bare hands.

For several years I studied karate and akido at Kim's Studio of Tae Kwon Do in Silver Spring, Maryland. I could kick opponents in the head, ribs and groin in a single rapid motion. I fought in matches, won trophies and learned how to throw people across the room, to take knives away from attackers, to split boards and crack slabs of marble.

The secret to breaking things lies largely in practice and utilizing principles of physics, but it is also a matter of concentration. You focus your energy on hitting a spot beyond the object you are striking. This technique worked for me in numerous karate demonstrations and tournaments. I liked smashing hostile cinder blocks; it gave me a real sense of power, security and being in control.

But one time my strong-man technique did not work.

I brought my new girlfriend to the dojo to show her another fascinating element of my mystique. I intended to thrill and impress her.

Setting up the cinder block, I made her stand back so she wouldn't get hit by flying fragments. I assumed my stance, focused and whacked the thing, expecting it to disintegrate. It didn't.

I hit it again.

Same result, but this time I think I heard a muffled giggle.

Then I really laid into that stupid gray block. Nothing. By now I was getting annoyed. I hit that target several more times. The obstinate thing still sat there, solid as a cinder block.

A fellow karate student came over and with one blow punched his way completely though the block, shattering it into a dozen jagged chunks.

I think God set me up for that one.

It's a shame that we can't learn humility without being humiliated. Anyhow, the young woman must have been more impressed with my soft head than with my hard hands, because she eventually did marry me. (And, to Ginny's everlasting credit, the other day while cleaning out a dusty storage box she discovered one of my old karate trophies and put it out for display without even mentioning the cinder block I could not break.)

Jesus never smashed a cinder block. He never resorted to amateur theatrics to demonstrate his strength. The one time he wanted to get through a stone, his living presence rolled it from the mouth of his tomb.

The Scriptures give us virtually no picture of the physical condition of Jesus. He may have been tall; he may have been short. He may have been a ninety-eight-pound weakling; he may have weighed three hundred pounds. Whether he was unable to carry the wooden beam of his cross as the result of the beating he received before the crucifixion or because it would have been just too heavy for his physical strength in the first place is a matter of pure conjecture.

In the Gospels, some people referred to him as a carpenter, indicating that he followed Joseph's trade for a time; but whether he was a cabinetmaker kind of carpenter or a construction-worker kind of carpenter we have no idea. Speaking prophetically, Isaiah says, "He had no beauty or majesty to attract us to him, nothing in his appearance that we should desire him" (Isaiah 53:2). I'm inclined to think Jesus was a bit on the hefty side, because his enemies accused him, without refute, of being a winebibber and a glutton. Being a fat guy myself, I take some comfort in that idea.

The word-portrait John paints in the beginning of Revelation shows a person of pulsating strength and power; this is the resurrected Lord and may not much resemble the "man of sorrows, acquainted with grief" who was seen by the people of New Testament times in Galilee. But the fact is that the power of Jesus lies beyond the physical realm.

The Power of God Declared in Scripture

Keeping in mind that the word *strength* means the power and ability to perform effectively, let's look at a few things the Scripture says concerning the strength of God, especially as it relates to prayer.

When the waters of the Red Sea closed over the chariots of Pharaoh, Moses sang the song recorded in Exodus 15. He rejoiced that God's power had thrown the horses and riders of the mightiest army on earth into the sea—gone in a puff.

Your right hand, O LORD,
     was majestic in power. . . .
By the blast of your nostrils
     the waters piled up. (vv. 6, 8)

In the midst of his troubles, Job said,

He spreads out the northern skies over empty space;
     he suspends the earth over nothing. . . .
The pillars of the heavens quake,
     aghast at his rebuke.
By his power he churned up the sea. . . .

And these are but the outer fringe of his works;
how faint the whisper we hear of him!
Who then can understand the thunder of his power?
(Job 26:7-14)

The prophet Isaiah declared that the earth is like a grasshopper before God, and that he gives kings and princes their energy to rule.

He who brings out the starry host one by one,
and calls them each by name.
Because of his great power and mighty strength,
not one of them is missing. . . .
The LORD is the everlasting God,
the Creator of the ends of the earth.
He will not grow tired or weary,
and his understanding no one can fathom.
He gives strength to the weary
and increases the power of the weak. (Isaiah 40:22-28)

St. Paul told the Ephesians that when we pray, God's power works in us, and he is able to do immeasurably more than all we ask or imagine. And the apostle John spoke for all Bible writers and said it all: "Hallelujah! For our Lord God Almighty reigns" (Revelation 19:6).

The Source of All Power

God, by definition, is infinite; if he had limits, he would be something less than God. Each of his characteristics, because they belong to him, are also without limit. If God has any power at all, he has all power without limit.

The Scriptures tell us again and again that God is the source of all power; that indeed he has the clout to do what he says he will. He is the source of power not just for ocean waves, storm clouds, lightning bolts and earthquakes but also for people.

Every person chooses how to use the energy God makes available to him or her. The electric company sees that the power is in the wires; we choose how to use it. We can heat our home, run a life-support system, microwave a pizza or watch MTV. We use the power of the electricity that runs through the wires—but we do not own it.

The source of all human strength is God. He formed the muscles and tendons of each of us in the womb. Hector, Alexander, Hercules, Samson, Rambo—all derive their physical prowess from their Creator. Each of us decides how to use the strength we have been given, but that strength comes from God.

Pornography star John Holmes claimed to have had intercourse with over a thousand different women before he died of AIDS in 1988. Now, I certainly hope he found mercy and peace in Christ before his death, but I doubt that John Holmes used his tremendous energy in the wisest possible manner while he was alive.

Water Power and Light
Thinking about God as the source of all power reminds me that once in a riot, I saw authorities use the power of water under pressure to disperse hundreds of people who did not want to be dispersed. I've seen zoo workers use that same water power to separate two fighting tigers. And I've seen firefighters tame the flames of a blazing building with a stream of water.

The point I want to make is that there is no more water at the nozzle end of the hose than there is at the faucet end. All the manifestations of power we see in nature—strong people, hurricanes, floods, erupting volcanoes—are drips at the nozzles of creation, the outer fringes of God's power. The Hydrant for all hoses is God.

He is the Living Water.

If I remember my physics correctly, the amount of energy/matter in the universe is constant; it changes form, but neither increases nor decreases itself.

A leaf transforms light energy into wood, which you can burn in your fireplace to generate heat. We ourselves are photo-dependent in that our energy originally comes from light. Blades of grass grow in sunlight, to be eaten by the cows, which become our burgers. No sunlight means no grass, which means no cows, which means no Big Macs.

And the Scripture says, "God is light; in him there is no darkness at all" (1 John 1:5).

Right off the bat he created light and separated it from darkness (Genesis 1:3-4).

Jesus said, "I am the light of the world" (John 8:12).

He is the source of all energy. In him we live and move and have our very being.

Making stars and critters and strong men in the past is a very impressive achievement. God is to be commended. But what about me and my prayer? If God has the ability to answer me and grant my request, why doesn't he?

— four —

Is God as Mean as a Snake?

If God is cruel,

then maybe he's just teasing

us when we pray.

G OD IS. GOD IS NEAR. HE HEARS OUR PRAYERS. HE HAS THE power to give us what we request. So why doesn't he?

Everyone who struggles with the question of why a prayer is not answered is tempted to wonder if perhaps God is something different from what we've been led to think. If God is good, and if, being an all-knowing God, he knows what we want or need before we even ask, then why doesn't he cooperate?

Sure he knows. The Bible says he knows every hair on your head; he knows every sparrow that falls; he knows every star and calls each one by name; he knows the thoughts and intents of the heart—and "your Father knows what you need before you ask him," Jesus said (Matthew 6:8).

And in a way, that makes the whole question of unanswered prayer all the more terrifying. What kind of Father is it who knows his children are in need, who hears them beg for help and who yet refuses to give the help they ask?

When we think along these lines, we are likely to conclude that God is like some earthly fathers—too mean to help his own children.

In Restoration London, back in the 1660s, dentists used the teeth of children to make dentures for wealthy clients, so some evil fathers pulled out all their own children's healthy teeth to sell for drinking money.

For some of us, thinking of God as a divine father does not inspire confidence. Many earthly fathers fall sadly short of heavenly, so we can well question just what kind of father God is.

We know that God reveals himself in the world he created. "For since the creation of the world God's invisible qualities—his eternal power and divine nature—have been clearly seen, being understood from what has been made" (Romans 1:20).

Well, what do we see when we look at what has been made? It depends on what you look at.

Big Fish Eat Little Ones

In Shakespeare's play *Pericles,* two fishermen stand on the deck of a ship, looking down into the water. One idly remarks, "Master, I marvel how the fishes live in the sea."

His companion answers, "Why, as men do aland; the great ones eat up the little ones."

We do live in a world where big fish eat little fish. Where deformed babies are born to wholesome young couples. Where little kids die of AIDS. Where petty tyrants threaten world peace. Where thousands lie down to sleep in gutters hungry every night. Where gangs of hoodlums beat up choirboys. Where old people languish neglected and lonely in nursing homes. Where brilliant students can't afford an education. Where chicken-hawk pimps snap up runaway children in bus terminals. Where centerfold bunnies earn more money than nurses. Where ministers get arrested on vice charges. Where snapping turtles pull under baby ducklings. Where drug pushers drive better cars than teachers. Where dirt makes newspaper headlines while heroic deeds go unreported.

Thinking about these things alone might bring a different shade of meaning to the old hymn "This Is My Father's World."

Outside my window last spring I watched a pair of downy woodpeckers diligently tap a hole for a nest in an old palm tree. The flash of sunlight on their red heads brought me joy. But no sooner was the nest built than a pair of ugly black grackles drove out the woodpeckers and took over the nest in a messy squabble.

What kind of Father made a world where the grackles win?

Once, walking along a river bank in a state park, I saw something black and silver thrashing in the water right at the edge where a little ditch emptied into the river. Fascinated, I drew closer and found thousands of fish fighting to get into the little ditch of water. The water boiled with them. They pressed each other so hard that the ones in back actually pushed the ones in the front ranks out of the water.

I asked a park ranger about this strange phenomenon, and he told me that a factory upriver was polluting the river, the little ditch contained fresh water and all those fish from the river were fighting to get into the ditch so they could breathe!

I cried.

Hard World = Hard God?

So what does nature as I observe it teach me about the character of God? Is the God who created this world a person I would trust to answer my prayers?

Okay. I know that the world in its present state lies under siege by sin. The Scripture tells me that Satan has usurped a place here and corrupts our whole planet. "For the creation was subjected to frustration, not by its own choice, but by the will of the one who subjected it, in hope that the creation itself will be liberated from its bondage to decay and brought into the glorious freedom of the children of God" (Romans 8:20-21).

That being so, why did Paul tell the Romans to look at the world to learn about God's eternal power and divine nature? It seems to me as though he would have told them to look at nature to see how mean and bad Satan is. But what we learn from God in nature depends on our own perspective.

Years ago, when I was driving a truck cross-country for a living, I made a delivery to the Air Force base in Dover, Delaware, and had to lay over a weekend in Odessa before I could pick up a return load. To pass the time I toured some of the lovely homes built by Quakers during colonial days. I wore my trucking-company uniform, and I must have looked relatively trustworthy, because in the garden of one home a vacationing family asked me to use their camera to take their picture against the backdrop of a rose arbor and fountain. The husband and wife were enjoying a second honeymoon with their young son. The little boy obviously doted on his daddy, and the woman clung to the man's arm and whispered tender nothings as they strolled in the garden.

The man told me he taught philosophy at an Ivy League university and just before vacation had been awarded tenure. He showed me a watch his students had given him as a token of their esteem and affection.

The couple asked me to watch their little boy while they toured a fine-crystal display in the kitchen of one of the old houses. So the kid and I hunted frogs by the fountain while the parents walked arm-in-arm through the exhibit, admiring antique glassware and furniture.

Later, the adults shared soft drinks on a balcony overlooking the gardens while the little boy played below, calling up now and then to show his daddy some prize butterfly he'd discovered. The professor and I got to talking about God.

He began to lecture me about the naiveté of Christianity in the face of natural evidence. Atheism is the only position any reasonable person can take, he assured me. He said that nature teaches us that if there is such a being as a god, it must be cold, harsh, cruel and capricious. He talked about big fish and little fish, deformed babies, wasted lives, polluted air, cancer, abusive parents and more such "evidence" from nature. He refuted arguments from teleology and cosmology and a bunch of other ologies I'd never heard of before. He soundly denounced the very idea of God.

All I could do was listen till he wound down. I really didn't know what to say in response to the pure force of his intellect. I doubt if I've ever talked with a smarter, better-educated man.

"That's really impressive," I said. "But I'd like to make one observation."

"What's that?"

"I've noticed that you are greatly loved. Your wife is obviously crazy about you. Your little boy worships you. Your colleagues at the university have honored you, and that watch tells me that your students hold you in high regard. Where did all that love around you come from? It has to have a source. Wherever there is love, there has to be a Lover."

I don't know how that idea popped out of my mouth. I thought the professor was going to cry.

He appeared to be absolutely smitten. "I've never thought of it like that before," he said.

His wife hugged him and laughed, "You ought to know better than to talk theology with a truck driver."

Well, sometimes God does use the weak and foolish to nudge the wise. The point I want to make here, though, is that while there is evil in the world, that's not all there is. There is love. There is nobility. There is selflessness. There is honesty. There is honor. There is beauty. There is goodness.

These things do have an origin.

Good Is

Oddly enough, evil makes the headlines because it is evil. By and large, goodness needs no publicity; it is so commonplace that we tend to overlook it.

Susannah Wesley, a Christian mother who lost ten of her nineteen children in infancy and who raised her remaining nine in abject, grueling poverty, said, "Though man is born to trouble, yet I believe there is scarce a man to be found upon earth but, take the whole course of his life, hath more mercies than afflictions, and much more pleasure than pain. I am sure it has been so in my case."

Yes indeed.

Taken as a whole, the lives of most people do contain more good days than bad. Even if you feel bitter about your own lot in life, think about it a bit; your bad days stand out because they are framed by normal, good, more or less contented days. This appears to be true for most of us.

We are saturated in goodness because God is good and the world he made is good, even though sin tries to spoil it.

Satan never laughs. He never enjoys anything. He gets no pleasure from ruining people. Demons have no fun. They gain nothing from destroying people. They act out of utter meanness. Sheer nastiness. Pure spite. Vile bitterness. Sneering contempt.

But even all their meanness only contaminates God's world: goodness is here. Goodness is the thing they pollute.

The trees are good trees. The grass is good grass. The rocks are good rocks. The sand is good sand. The air and rain and seas and rivers are naturally good. Pollution is not their natural state.

The Scriptures tell us again and again that God is good. The very first chapter of the Bible uses the word *good* over and over. God saw that the light was good; that the waters and the dry land were good; that the fields and the trees were good; that the day and the night were good; that the great whales and the winged fowl, the creeping things and the beasts of the forests, the man and the woman were good. And when you read to the end of the chapter, where God surveys everything he had made, you find him admiring it all: "Indeed it was *very* good" (Genesis 1:31 NKJV).

At the end of the story of Joseph in Egypt (Genesis 50), after his brothers had knocked him in the head, dumped him in a pit and sold him for a slave, and after God finally delivered him, Joseph forgave his brothers and told them, "You intended to harm me, but God intended it for good" (v. 20).

When St. Peter spoke to Cornelius, a Roman centurion, he said, "You know . . . how God anointed Jesus of Nazareth with the Holy Spirit and power, and how he went around doing good" (Acts 10:37-38). The eleventh verse of John's third epistle simply states, "He who does good is of God." A quick check of my handy vest-pocket edition of *Strong's Exhaustive Concordance to the Holy Scriptures* (which lists every word in the Bible along with each one's Hebrew or Greek roots) shows that the word *good* occurs 705 times in the Bible; the word *bad* occurs 17 times. You suppose that's why they call it "the Good Book"?

A person who cannot tell the difference between good and bad, between right and wrong, is judged to be legally insane. You'd have to be crazy not to know what good is; but just to be sure, I checked my dictionary to see. There's a huge entry defining the word *good,* and virtually every shade of meaning dovetails with character traits that theologians refer to as attributes of God!

Good means "of a favorable character, certain to last, wholesome, deserving respect, honorable, setting a standard, kind, benevolent, upper-class, competent, of the highest worth, well-behaved, conforming to the moral order of the universe, praiseworthy, healthy, having intrinsic value, permanent, giving the best results, an affable companionable person, having a generous disposition, cheerful, attractive, cooperative, marked by principles of friendship, supportive, agreeable, pleasant"—and the list goes on!

When we say God is good, we mean all that—infinitely. Without limit.

A God of Pleasure

Once when Jesus told his disciples to sell all they owned and give to the poor, he prefaced this with the words "Do not fear, little flock, for it is your Father's good pleasure to give you the kingdom" (Luke 12:32 NKJV).

Every healthy thing, everything you truly enjoy, every pleasure you feel, every bit of fun, every smile, every laugh, every joy—all these things come from the hand of God, untwisted by sin. "Every good and perfect gift is from above, coming down from the Father of the heavenly lights, who does not change like shifting shadows," said the apostle James (James 1:17).

Yes, God is the source of all pleasure: King David rejoiced,

You will show me the path of life;

In Your presence is fullness of joy;

At Your right hand are pleasures forevermore. (Psalm 16:11 NKJV)

Pleasures forevermore!

A good God, giving good and perfect gifts because it is *his* good pleasure for *us* to enjoy good pleasure. When we pray for good things we echo God's will for us, because he also wants good things, the best, for us.

Now I'm not advocating a Pollyanna worldview, that this is the best of all possible worlds. It ain't—yet. But I do believe that the underlying world structure created by God shows that the Creator is good.

Why Do We Expect Good?

Strangely enough, in spite of all the bad nasties we see around us, virtually all of our expectations argue that God is good.

When a used-car dealer palms a clunker off on you, you feel

frustrated, outraged, disappointed and cheated. Why? Because you expected good. And when that good does not come, you know that it should have. Some internal sense causes you to expect good. You didn't get that internal sense from observing that big fish eat little ones. Good is what ought to be. Everyone knows that. And we know that something is out of whack when bad happens; we all act as though good were the norm for the whole world system. Yes, we do fear evil and protect ourselves against it as best we are able, but we really expect good and are disappointed if it does not come about.

And, in fact, good people abound. The woods are full of them. Not a day goes by that some firefighter does not risk life and limb to save a stranger, motivated by something more than the wish to hold onto a good civil service job. Police officers put their lives on the line to protect others. Nurses risk horrible infections to care for the sick. Parents work night and day to provide for their children. Child-care workers put up with obnoxious brats day in and day out because even brats need care.

The world abounds with good, caring people and when one shirks duty or falls into corruption, that dereliction is so unusual that it makes the headlines. Could it be that the bad guys make the front pages because they are the *exception?*

There's no doubt that ours is a sinful, fallen race, but despite our first parents' fall into sin, the bad nasties that plague society— the tyranny of Satan over our world, pollution, AIDS, abortion, nuclear weapons and sitcoms—the original underlying good of the Creator cannot be erased from his creation.

God Our Father

Despite fathers who pull all the kids' teeth, dads who abandon the family for some floozie, deadbeat dads who skip their child-support payments, dads who never look up from the TV, *Father* is still the term Jesus uses of God when he prays.

But that certainly doesn't mean Jesus was ignorant of how bad earthly fathers can be. He once asked the gang, "If a child asks for fish, or for bread to eat, will you give him a scorpion, a snake or a rock?" He knew full well that some fathers might do just that. After all, when Jesus himself was born, the king of his nation was Herod, who had killed most of his own sons—some by poisoning, some by starvation. Everyone in the crowd Jesus was addressing knew that Caesar had said of this Jewish king, "It's safer to be Herod's pig than Herod's son."

Even knowing all that, Jesus still uses the term *Father*. He told the crowd, "If you, then, though you are evil, know how to give good gifts to your children, how much more will your Father in heaven give good gifts to those who ask him!" (Matthew 7:11).

But I'm still confused. When I pray and don't see an answer, I still wonder what's wrong. I mean, if there is a God, and if he is available, and if he is able to help me, and if he is a kind and loving Father, but nothing happens when I pray—I just don't understand.

Jesus did promise that when we pray, we'll be sure to get an answer. Didn't he?

— five —

Prayer: What It Ain't, What It Is

If I'm not really praying,

can I look for an answer?

WHEN JENNIFER, MY OLDEST DAUGHTER, WAS TINY, FOUR OR five years old, she played with an imaginary playmate named Lisa. During our family prayers each night, Jennifer insisted that we pray for the imaginary troubles of the imaginary Lisa.

Every night Jennifer announced the latest Lisa dilemma: "Lisa is going to Africa as a missionary . . . Lisa needs new clothes . . . Lisa is pregnant . . . Lisa is getting married . . . Lisa wants a Barbie doll . . . Lisa got run over by a car . . . Lisa has cancer; let's pray for her."

This presented me with a dilemma: Should I encourage this behavior? Is it proper to pray about such imaginary troubles?

As I pondered the question, an odd but comforting thought impressed itself on my mind: *Relax, John, just about every worry you yourself pray over is imaginary too!*

Obviously there's a difference between imagining and praying, but our family continued to "pray" for Lisa until a kitten replaced her in Jennifer's affections.

Jennifer is now married to Mike, a fireman, and she works as a registered nurse in a charity hospital, where she cares for AIDS and crack babies. She was not always so compassionate. During family devotions one night when she was in second grade, she prayed earnestly, "Dear Jesus, please make Joey get real sick so I can have his part in the school play."

She obviously learned to pray like that from me. Although I have learned to couch my prayers in more refined wording, often I have vocalized the same sort of selfish sentiment when I wanted something.

Are our selfish, greedy sentiments really prayers? When we question why a specific prayer of ours has not been answered, one question we need to ask ourselves is *Have I really been praying, or have I merely been imagining things—or just wishing?*

John—Slim and Trim

For instance, I wish I could lose weight. But I have not prayed to Almighty God about losing weight.

You see, it would be kind of nice to regain my sleek boyish figure, to lounge on the beach without being self-conscious, to draw admiring glances from young women. I'd like that. I even say now and then, "I'd like to lose about thirty pounds"; but I'd like to lose that weight overnight, without any discomfort to myself.

I wish I were magically, immediately slim and trim.

I have not prayed to lose weight.

Knowing what I do of God, I suspect that if I were to ask him to help me lose weight, he'd put me on a diet. He'd take away my Twinkies. He'd deprive me of Pepsi. He'd cut off my Pringles. He'd feed me celery. He might even make me exercise!

In other words, God would actually take my request seriously.

More seriously than I do myself.

Are you wishing, or are you praying?

Wish or Pray?

Now, there is nothing wrong with wishing and daydreaming. But we should recognize the difference between those activities and praying.

To wish is to have a desire for something, but it is a relatively weak desire. The term *wishy-washy* shows how lacking in strength that desire is. We'd like to believe that such and such will happen; but we don't much expect it to, and while it would be nice, we certainly don't intend to work to make it happen.

A wish is uttered into the air. It is seldom directed toward anyone in particular. A prayer, on the other hand, is specifically addressed to Someone.

Webster's defines *pray* as "to entreat, to implore, to make an earnest plea." A prayer expresses a strong desire, a real lack, an urgent request. There is nothing wishy-washy about it. Prayer concerns something you really want, something important to you, something you really care about.

Unfortunately, I find that I often drift into mouthing vague good wishes when I think that I am praying. You know the kind of thing I mean: "And bless the missionaries in Africa. And help the doctors doing AIDS research. And fix the economy. And the guys in prison. And Randy and Lisa. And the U.S. Olympic teams. And the whole state of Christ's church and the world . . . Oh yes, and Sheba's new puppies too."

And while I feel pious from having done my duty in prayer, I doubt if that sort of vaporizing racks up many points with God.

Another thing I sometimes substitute for prayer is worry. To worry is to repeatedly agitate a subject mentally, to give that subject persistent, nagging attention. The word *worry* originally meant to constrict, choke or strangle; it was used of a dog shaking a rat in its teeth. When something worries me, I'm the said squeaking rat, and my "prayer" runs something like this:

Dear God, they are going to cut our lights off if I don't pay that bill by Thursday. And payday isn't till next week. And the hamburger in the freezer will spoil. But maybe we can eat it Thursday afternoon. Or if it begins to turn, we can feed it to Sheba. Maybe we'll have to, because I forgot that the stove is electric too and we won't have any way to cook. I'll get out the charcoal grill, and we can cook on the back porch. That's it. Make a picnic out of it. Have to do something like that to keep the kids amused, because they won't be able to watch TV. Maybe I'll read to them some. But if we don't have electricity, we won't have lights either.

I know, I'll get out some candles. Better be careful; if one gets knocked over, the house could catch fire. Then we'd really be in a fix. All the clothes gone and us standing out in the street in our underwear with blankets over our shoulders and my hairy legs sticking out. And with my books all burned up, how would I work? And the landlord will have me arrested for cooking on a grill inside. But if we don't cook it, the hamburger will spoil. And even if we feed it to Sheba, it might make her sick all over the rug. And we can't shampoo it, because that takes electricity too. And if I ask Mrs. Herschel, the old busybody, to keep it in her freezer, she'll know that our lights are off and she'll . . .

I can spend hours in "prayer" like that.

Worry focuses on the problem; wishing seldom focuses at all; prayer focuses on Jesus.

What *Did* Jesus Promise?

Let's look at some of the things Jesus taught about prayer in the four Gospels. First, two passages from his Sermon on the Mount:

When you pray, go into your room, close the door and pray to your Father, who is unseen. Then your Father, who sees what is done in secret, will reward you. And when you pray, do not keep on babbling like pagans, for they think they will be heard because of their many words. Do not be like them, for your Father knows what you need before you ask him. (Matthew 6:6-8)

Ask and it will be given to you; seek and you will find; knock and the door will be opened to you. For everyone who asks receives; he who seeks finds; and to him who knocks, the door will be opened.

Which of you, if his son asks for bread, will give him a stone? Or if he asks for a fish, will give him a snake? If you, then, though you are evil, know how to give good gifts to your children, how much more will your Father in heaven give good gifts to those ask him! (Matthew 7:7-11)

These words were addressed to the disciples within the hearing of a large crowd of other people. The promises Christ makes are comprehensive, the conditions he mentions are few. We are to pray in secret, behind closed doors. God who sees in secret will reward. We don't need to babble, because God knows what we ask even before we begin praying.

Ask and it will be given. Whoever asks receives. Prayer demonstrates our child-Father relationship with God. Like the best of earthly fathers, the Father will give good gifts to his children who ask; he certainly gives nothing less than what they ask for.

Figs and Faith

Mark's Gospel tells how Jesus cursed a barren fig tree and how amazed the disciples were. Speaking to the twelve, Jesus then said:

Have faith in God. . . . I tell you the truth, if anyone says to this mountain, 'Go, throw yourself into the sea,' and does not doubt in his heart but believes that what he says will happen, it will be done for him. Therefore I tell you, whatever you ask for in prayer, believe that you have received it, and it will be yours. And when you stand praying, if you hold anything against anyone, forgive him, so that your Father in heaven may forgive you your sins. (Mark 11:22-25)

Again we see the sweeping scope of prayer—"whatever you ask for"—and two important conditions: We can ask for anything without limit and it will be ours—*if* we ask in faith and *if* we forgive. Jesus repeated these two conditions for answered prayer often, but the one he emphasized most was forgiving others.

Notice the strong link between forgiving and praying: "if you hold anything against anyone." Here again the child-Father relationship shows up: we are to forgive as our Father does.

The Petitions of a Pest

In Luke's Gospel, just after Jesus told his disciples about his Second Coming, he taught them another lesson about prayer.

Then Jesus told his disciples a parable to show them that they should always pray and not give up. He said, "In a certain town there was a judge who neither feared God nor cared about men. And there was a widow in that town who kept coming to him with the plea, 'Grant me justice against my adversary.'

"For some time he refused. But finally he said to himself, 'Even though I don't fear God or care about men, yet because this widow keeps bothering me, I will see that she gets justice, so that she won't eventually wear me out with her coming!' "

And the Lord said, "Listen to what the unjust judge says. And will not God bring about justice for his chosen ones, who cry out to him day and night? Will he keep putting them off? I tell you, he will see that they get justice, and quickly. However, when the Son of Man comes, will he find faith on the earth?" (Luke 18:1-8)

Jesus often described God in terms of earthly examples which in the mouth of anyone else might seem irreverent—a thief in the night, a dead body where vultures gather, an unjust judge. In this prayer parable, we see an uncaring man worn down by a woman's persistent asking; will God keep putting us off?

Even when our prayers seem to get nowhere, Jesus teaches that we are not to give up. When we do not see an immediate answer, the temptation is to despair of ever getting any answer; but as the old proverb goes, "God may not answer when you want him to, but when he does, he's never late!"

Holy Prayer, Unholy Life

Luke says that one day when Jesus was teaching the general public in the temple courtyard, some of the big shots of the day badgered him with heckling questions regarding John the Baptist, paying taxes, resurrection and marriage. Jesus used that occasion to teach another important element of prayer. "While all the people were listening, Jesus said to his disciples, 'Beware of the teachers of the law. They like to walk around in flowing robes and love to be greeted in the marketplaces and have the most important seats in the synagogues and the places of honor at banquets. They devour widows' houses and for a show make lengthy prayers. Such men will be punished most severely" (Luke 20:45-47).

Punished for praying?

Yes. Here Jesus links prayer with an honest lifestyle. What we think of as shrewd business practices can certainly turn our prayers to curses on our own heads! We can legally take advantage of the poor, the underprivileged, the orphan and widow. We can legally turn a profit in the slums. We can turn aside from the homeless. But then even long prayers will not turn aside our great damnation.

You can't live a goat and die a lamb.

A total Christian lifestyle must be linked with Christian prayer. So trust and do. Trust in the Lord and do good.

Two Things to Pray For

Luke says that shortly after the above teaching, perhaps even the same evening, the disciples pointed out to Jesus the beauty of the temple, and he foretold Jerusalem's destruction and his own coming again in a cloud with power and great glory. Then he said this concerning prayer: "Be careful, or your hearts will be weighed down with dissipation, drunkenness and the anxieties of life, and that day will close on you unexpectedly like a trap. For it will come upon all those who live on the face of the whole earth. Be always on the watch, and pray that you may be able to escape all that is about to happen, and that you may be able to stand before the Son of Man" (Luke 21:34-36).

We are to pray to escape and to stand. We are to pray about the general deterioration we see around us daily. I frequently use the TV evening news as a prompter for prayer about how fouled up this world is, about drunkenness, drug addiction and the general emptiness life holds for people living godless lives.

We are to pray about the anxieties of life; you know enough about those already.

We are to pray that we may escape these things. We are to pray to escape the effects of them, and that we may not contribute to them, so that we will be able to stand before Jesus when he returns.

Again we see that Jesus links the general tenor of our lives to our prayers. To pray Christian, we must live Christian. Trust and do.

Andrew Murray, author of *The Prayer Life,* said, "The prayer life is not something which can be improved by itself. It is so intimately bound up with the entire spiritual life that it is only when that whole life becomes renewed and sanctified that prayer can have its rightful place of power. We must not be satisfied with less than the victorious life to which God calls his children."

If We Pray, What Then?

John's Gospel tells that during the Last Supper, after Jesus

washed the disciples' feet and Judas left, Jesus spoke at length
about the coming of the Comforter, about heaven and about prayer:
I tell you the truth, anyone who has faith in me will do what I
have been doing. He will do even greater things than these,
because I am going to the Father. And I will do whatever you
ask in my name, so that the Son may bring glory to the Father.
You may ask me for anything in my name, and I will do it. (John
14:12-14)
I am the vine; you are the branches. If a man remains in me
and I in him, he will bear much fruit; apart from me you can do
nothing. . . . If you remain in me and my words remain in you,
ask whatever you wish, and it will be given you. (John 15:5, 7)
You did not choose me, but I chose you and appointed you to
go and bear fruit—fruit that will last. Then the Father will give
you whatever you ask in my name. This is my command: Love
each other. (John 15:16-17)
Now is your time of grief, but I will see you again and you will
rejoice, and no one will take away your joy. In that day you will
no longer ask me anything. I tell you the truth, my Father will
give you whatever you ask in my name. Until now you have not
asked for anything in my name. Ask and you will receive, and
your joy will be complete. (John 16:22-24)
Flabbergasting!
Whatever! Whatever! Whatever!
Anything! Anything! Anything!
Ask! Ask! Ask! Ask whatever you wish!
Nothing imaginary, worrisome or wishy-washy about this kind
of prayer.
I will do whatever you ask in my name. . . . I will do it. . . . It will
be given you. . . . The Father will give you whatever you ask in my
name. . . . Ditto. . . . Ask and you will receive, and your joy will be
complete.
Wow!

We are to abide, remain, love, bear fruit, ask. Ask in Jesus' name.

Now, we should not get hung up on the phrase "in Jesus' name." There is no secret formula here; it is simply that on the basis of our relationship with him we can be bold to approach the very throne of God expecting to be well received. As Christ-ones, we already do ask in Jesus' name.

I have talked with some deeply spiritual Christians who have almost abandoned the literal meaning of the words John records. They seem to feel that prayer means being aware of God's presence, that we should focus on achieving a mystic communion with God and that simple asking for things is an inferior, childish kind of prayer.

Do you see that idea in the sections of Jesus' teachings we've just read? Is that what Jesus taught?

But then I've talked with other Christians who seem to feel that God is obligated to give them all the trappings of success and business prosperity because they have prayed for this stuff.

Is *that* what Jesus taught?

From my reading of the four Gospels, it looks to me as though Jesus didn't have an awful lot to say about achieving spiritual ecstasy through prayer, at least to the point that material stuff would drop out of our prayers altogether. On the other hand, what kind of prosperity did Jesus himself enjoy? Foxes have dens and birds have nests, but Jesus didn't exactly live in the 90210 zip-code section of Jerusalem. He sat in somebody else's boat to teach. He rode someone else's donkey in his triumphal entry. His cross was government property. He borrowed a tomb to be buried in (and he returned it hardly used). Asking for and receiving material things apparently played little part in his prayer life.

All this confuses me.

When I have prayed, I have hardly ever felt the overwhelming presence of the Lord God Almighty, High and Lifted Up, the

Numinous, the scary presence of pure Holiness that would make me lie face-down on the floor saying, "Depart from me, for I am a sinful man."

Neither have I gotten all that many goodies when I've asked for them.

Sometimes I feel like Christian chopped liver. Do you suppose that God is mad at me?

— six —

Sweet Prayers to an Angry God

If God is holy,

will he answer the prayers

of a sinner like me?

T HE IDEA OF PRAYING TO A *GOOD* FATHER IN HEAVEN SEEMS strange to many modern Americans. Don't preachers harp on hell and damnation? Isn't our traditional view of God one of a harsh, stern, legalistic Law-Enforcer frowning down on the earth, just waiting to catch somebody having fun?

Jonathan Edwards, one of the most famous Puritan preachers, takes what I think is a bum rap for this view in some history books. They say he advocated such a mean view of God; did he really?

Of all the Christian sermons ever preached, only three have achieved any sort of general fame: Christ's Sermon on the Mount, St. Francis's "Sermon to the Birds" and Jonathan Edwards's "Sinners in the Hands of an Angry God." Edwards preached this message at Enfield, Connecticut, on July 8, 1741. His text was Deuteronomy 32:35, "Their foot shall slide in due time."

In this sermon, Edwards compares an unconverted person to a

spider dangling on a flimsy thread above a fire. "Unconverted men walk over the pit of hell on a rotten covering," Edwards said, "And there are innumerable places in this covering so weak that they will not bear their weight, and these places are not seen. . . . There is nothing between you and hell but air; it is only the power and mere pleasure of God that holds you up. If God should withdraw his hand, nothing would avail to keep you from falling."

He said that God does not need to cast sinners into hell; our own wickedness makes us as heavy as lead, and our own weight presses us downward. Only God's love can hold up such a heavy weight and keep us from falling. "If God should let you go, you would sink immediately and swiftly descend and plunge into the bottomless gulf, and your healthy constitution, and all your righteousness, would have no more influence to uphold you and keep you out of hell than a spider's web would have to stop a falling rock. Were it not for the sovereign pleasure of God, the earth would not bear you one moment." The people who originally heard this sermon became so frightened, so convicted of their sin, that they screamed and grabbed hold of each other and the church seats to keep from falling into hell.

The point Edwards made again and again in his famous sermon is that it is only God's love and mercy that keeps us from dropping down, carried under by our own weight.

Sinners in the Arms of a Loving God

Did Edwards see God as a Big Meanie, cruel and capricious? How would a mean God answer prayer?

Let's peek at Edwards's inner thoughts about the God to whom he prayed. In the winter of 1739 he wrote *A Personal Narrative,* in which he tried to express the delight he felt in prayer:

> The first instance that I remember of that sort of inward, sweet delight in God and divine things that I have lived much in since, was on reading the words, I Tim i. 17, *Now unto the King eternal,*

immortal, invisible, the only wise God, be honor and glory for ever and ever, Amen. As I read the words, there came into my soul, and was as it were diffused through it, a sense of the glory of the Divine Being; a new sense, quite different from any thing I ever experienced before. . . . I thought with myself, how excellent a Being that was, and how happy I should be, if I might enjoy that God, and be rapt up to him in heaven, and be as it were swallowed up in him for ever! . . .

From about that time, I began to have a new kind of apprehensions and ideas of Christ, and the work of redemption, and the glorious way of salvation by him. An inward, sweet sense of these things, at times came into my heart; and my soul was led away in pleasant views and contemplations of them. And my mind was greatly engaged to spend my time in reading and meditating on Christ, on the beauty and excellency of his person, and the lovely way of salvation by free grace in him. . . .

The sense I had of divine things would often of a sudden kindle up, as it were, a sweet burning in my heart; an ardor of soul that I know not how to express. . . .

The appearance of every thing was altered; there seemed to be, as it were, a calm, sweet cast, or appearance of divine glory, in almost every thing. God's excellency, his wisdom, his purity and love, seemed to appear in every thing; in the sun, moon, and stars; in the clouds, and blue sky; in the grass, flowers, trees; in the water, and all nature; which used greatly to fix my mind. I often used to . . . behold the sweet glory of God in these things. . . . I was almost constantly in ejaculatory prayer wherever I was. Prayer seemed to be natural to me as the breath by which the inward burnings of my heart had vent.

Does that sound to you as though Edwards worshiped a harsh, mean God? For page after page, Edwards tries to articulate his enjoyment of Christ. One single page is sprinkled with words and phrases such as "wonder . . . wondrous . . . rejoiced . . . glorious . . .

exalting . . . pleasant . . . the pleasantest thing of all . . . rejoiced . . . entertained and delighted . . . sense of excellent fullness of Christ . . . swallowed up in Christ . . . extraordinary glory of the Son of God . . . ineffably excellent." In virtually every paragraph on that page, Edwards uses the word *sweet* six or eight times!

A visitor in the Edwards home, a twenty-six-year-old bachelor, felt astounded at the happiness of Jonathan, his wife Sarah and their eleven children; he uses the word *sweet* to describe what he found in that family. One diary entry says:

Sunday, October 19, 1740—Felt great satisfaction in being at the house of Mr. Edwards. A sweeter couple I have not yet seen. Their children [are] examples of Christian simplicity. Mrs. Edwards is adorned with a meek and quiet spirit . . . such a helpmate to her husband.

Contact with the happy Edwards family caused the bachelor "to renew those prayers which, for some months, I have put up to God that He would be pleased to send me a daughter of Abraham to be my wife!"

Virtually everything about this happy Puritan preacher indicates that far from being a sour grouch worshiping a mean God, he found incredible sweetness in a loving God.

But if God is sweet and good, then what about all those dire warnings in the Bible? The unquenchable thirst, the lake of fire, the place of torment, where the worm never dies—those warnings scattered all through the Bible sound pretty bad, don't they?

The Horn Blows a Warning

When Ginny and I were first engaged, I drove a brand-new 1967, four-on-the-floor (I don't think they even had automatic transmissions back then) Mustang. Bright yellow, the yellow you only see nowadays edging the cover of a *National Geographic* magazine. Wow! A sporty new car and a beautiful woman. Wasn't I something!

On Christmas Eve, Ginny wanted a few last-minute things from the mall, and I was proud to drive her in spite of the heavy traffic. Turning left off the main highway into the mall, we got stuck in a monster line of plain, drab old cars which inched up a steep hill and trickled past the traffic light one or two at a time. We were obviously going to be stuck in traffic on that hill for a while, and since even back then I was a biblically minded man, I decided to "redeem the time." So whenever the line of traffic stopped, I reached for Ginny, or she reached for me, and we smooched fervently.

HONK! Honk-honk!

What's this? The guy behind me kept hitting his horn, the creep. *What's the matter with him? Traffic isn't going anywhere.* We started kissing again. Again, he started honking.

The spoilsport. Let him find his own girl. What business is it of his what I do in the privacy of my own new yellow four-on-the-floor Mustang?

The light changed. I crept forward in the line maybe three car lengths and stopped again. Again we kissed; again he honked. He not only honked, he also flashed his lights at me!

Now I was getting mad. This guy was a pest, a creep, a voyeur, a busybody. *I've half a mind to . . .*

The traffic light changed again. I inched up the hill toward the turnoff and stopped on red to resume smooching. The dirty so-and-so really leaned on his horn this time. But I ignored the killjoy and kept on kissing until—*crunch!*

Here, younger readers should know that a car with a manual transmission requires that the driver keep one foot on the brake and the other on the clutch when the car is stopped on a hill in traffic. If you don't do that, then your car rolls backward.

That's what I had done. Yes, every time I'd leaned over to kiss Ginny, I had let up on both clutch and brake until I rolled backward and smacked into the driver behind me, the one who had done everything in his power to warn me of the danger.

I did not feel quite so sporty when I had to get out of the car and apologize to him. I felt stupid and silly—and I discovered that I'd crumpled my own rear end (you can take that figuratively *and* literally).

Now let me say straight out that as a Christian I have nothing against engaged couples kissing. I wish them joy. However, I'd be a dunce if I did not learn from my own experience that when God warns me about something he's not being a spoilsport, a killjoy or a busybody meddling in affairs which are no concern of his. If the Scripture teaches nothing else, it teaches that God hates to see his children get hurt. So he warns us. He warns us again and again. He blows the horn and blinks the lights when we do certain things because he can see that if we keep it up we are going to crumple our own rear ends.

But most of us do just as I did with that other driver: we ignore the danger signs or get peeved at the person doing the warning.

God's Laws and God's Holiness

Cars roll downhill when the driver is not keeping one foot on the brake. And there are other principles of law in the universe. These rules are not arbitrary. God's rules are absolute.

Take an easy one: God's rule against stealing. In general, the Bible teaches that if something is not yours, leave it alone. The rule absolutely applies to everyone, because God is absolutely holy. His absolute rules arise out of his own holy nature, and these rules are designed to keep us from getting hurt.

When we break God's rule about stealing, we do not injure God. We do not even do irreparable damage to the person we steal from. We are the ones who are damaged by our own breaking of God's rules.

When my children were small, I absolutely commanded them not to bathe the cat in our bathtub. Their putting the cat in the water would not hurt me. It would not hurt the cat. Who would get scratched? The answer to that became clear when the kids broke my commandment. Their howls sounded as if they came from sinners in the claws of an angry cat!

The horrible consequences of breaking God's rules do not indicate that God is a big meanie who can not be approached in prayer. Actually, the consequences of breaking God's rules are natural phenomena, effects of a cause, not the gleeful torments of a divine torturer.

If you steal, you become a thief. If you murder, you become a murderer. If you slip around on your spouse, you become a cheat. You are the person who is damaged, degraded, hurt.

And God hates to see one of his children damaged, degraded and hurt. So God's Word warns us not to steal. Stealing makes us thieves, and God doesn't want to see that happen to one of his beloved ones. And that's just what you and I are—beloved ones of God.

Christ warned and warned us away from the sins that bring us down, defeat us and corrupt us. Then he died to save us from the sin that has us beat. He died the death for us and rose again from that death to lift us up to where he is.

Amazing? What can we say after all that?

Unfortunately, most of us don't say much. We're too proud to say thank you to God, or to repeat his warnings even to the people we care about most.

I suspect that most people do just as I did that Christmas Eve when I ignored the warnings. I fussed and fumed and blamed—and then ended up driving around with my rear end crumpled.

Nobody should live like that.

St. Paul was not speaking tongue in cheek when he linked two rules for living in 1 Thessalonians 5:14: in one breath he told Christians to "warn them that are unruly," and in the next he commanded, "Comfort the feeble-minded" (KJV).

Sometimes I feel like both edges of that verse apply to me—and I don't mean that I'm the one doing the warning or the comforting.

So?

So if God is holy and knows how to give good gifts to those who ask him, I still want to know why I don't get the good things I ask him for.

— seven —

Maybe God
Just Doesn't Care

If God does not like me,

will he answer my prayers?

G OD IS.
God is near.

God invites us to pray.

God is able to answer our prayers.

God is good. God is Father. God is kind and not cruel.

God is holy. God hates to see people hurt.

I believe all these things are true. But I still puzzle over the question of why so many of my own specific prayers are not answered. My daily experiences conflict with my beliefs. The tension between the two leaves me in a quandary. I believe. I pray—and yet I hurt.

What's wrong?

A creeping suspicion arises in my mind: could it be that God loves people in general, but does not answer my prayers because he doesn't have much use for me in particular?

The Bible tells me that the answer to this horrible suspicion lies in the cross of Jesus.

Of Jewelry, the Cross and Fire

The only piece of jewelry I own is a tie clasp shaped like a hammer. My grandfather gave it to me for my eleventh birthday. He had won it as a prize for a project he submitted to some carpentry magazine's woodworking contest. The silver plating wore off it years ago, but I still treasure my little hammer. Nevertheless, I do not believe Christians should own or wear jewelry. I view jewelry as a gaudy vanity smacking of worldliness.

Naturally, everyone else in my family views me as a party-pooping, hopelessly out-of-date old fogy. They bedeck themselves with all sorts of costume ornaments, tacky baubles, glittery rings, shiny plastic pins, ropes of multicolored beads, sparkling things shaped like dead fish that dangle from their ears.

And every one of them often wears some kind of cross—filigree crosses, Celtic crosses, glass crosses, embroidered crosses, etc., etc.

Even my six-foot-three, broad-as-a-door teenage son wears a cross. It hangs on a long rawhide thong. Donald's cross consists of two heavy, square-cut iron nails, welded together at right angles.

He says that a cross symbolizes God's love, and that looking at a cross as he prays helps him remember to pray in five areas: The head of the cross reminds him to adore Christ. The left arm reminds him to confess sins; the right arm, to thank God for the good things in life. The point where the timbers intersect reminds him to pray for the people whose lives cross his own. And the foot of the cross is the place to lay burdens and make requests known to God.

Now, in order to conserve money (for the family to throw away on more jewelry, I suppose), we heat our home by burning wood. We have a big fireplace, and here in Florida wood is certainly cheaper than fuel oil.

For a fire to burn, it needs three things: a source of heat to start with, fuel and oxygen. Without all three it smolders and peters out. Of course in our house, everybody likes to feel the fire's warmth but nobody likes to feed the fire. So one day last winter, the fire died down to a glowing bed of coals.

To build it up again, Donald chunked on a few more logs. It started smoking up the room. As a certified genius and a nuclear-physics major with a full academic scholarship to college, Donald realized the problem was lack of oxygen. He got down on his hands and knees to blow into the fireplace as the rest of the family stood around offering helpful suggestions like "Hurry up! It's cold in here!" and "Move. Your big butt blocks all the heat."

Ignoring our help, Donald pushed his head deeper into the fireplace to blow on the coals; and as he did, that cross of iron nails dangled out of his shirt and nested in the glowing embers.

At last the fire reignited. Donald stood up. Grabbing the leather thong, he dropped the cross back down inside his shirt . . .

When that hot cross touched his bare skin, he hollered and danced and pounded his chest like Conan the Barbarian on a roll. We all saw it happen. And as a nurturing Christian family, filled with compassion, harmony, tenderheartedness and love for one another, we laughed ourselves silly at his pain while we called out words of charity and comfort ranging from "You're on fire for the Lord!" to "You dweeb!"

Donald claims that this "suffering for the faith" entitles him to be considered a card-carrying Christian martyr. By now his scars have healed, but he still wears that cross as a symbol of his faith and as a reminder to pray. So the cross can stand for our faith. But it also symbolizes other things, including God's love for us.

God's Love and Pain
In an earlier chapter I said that we don't know what Jesus actually looked like. And we don't. But archaeologists have discovered one

very ancient picture representing him. It may have been drawn as
early as forty or so years after Christ's crucifixion and resurrection.

After the great fire of Rome in A.D. 64, Emperor Nero built a new

Used by permission of *Christian History*.

palace, which he named "The Golden House," on Palatine Hill, northeast of the Colosseum. And that, as you recall, was where Christians, accused of setting the fire, were fed to the lions. The Roman writer Suetonius describes Nero's magnificent palace:

Its vestibule was large enough to contain a colossal statue of the Emperor a hundred and twenty feet high; and it was so extensive that it had a triple colonnade a mile long. There was a pond too, like a sea, surrounded with buildings to represent cities, besides tracts of country, varied by tilled fields, vineyards, pastures and woods, with great numbers of wild and domestic animals. In the rest of the house, all parts were overlaid with gold and adorned with gems and mother-of-pearl.

Close to the Golden House Nero constructed another building, called the Paedagogium. It housed imperial offices as well as barracks, rooms where palace guards and gladiators lived while on duty. The soldiers liked to scratch rough pictures and slogans, called graffiti, into the plaster walls of their barracks—you know the sort of thing, the first-century equivalent of "Call Diana for a good time . . . Sarge is a fink . . . Less filling; tastes great."

In 1856, among these drawings Italian antiquarian R. Garrucci discovered a picture graffito with the inscription "Alexamenos worships his God." This picture, now housed in Rome's Museo Kircheriano, is the earliest known portrait of the crucifixion. It shows a small man, Alexamenos, praying; he stands with one arm extended toward our Savior, who is suffering on the cross. The cross appears to be a Tau cross, shaped like a capital *T,* with a title board on top. Our Lord's feet rest on a small shelf or crossbar, his body is taut, his arms stretch out on the hard wood of the cross with the nails visible in his hands.

In this crude picture, scratched on the barracks wall by some pagan soldier, Jesus has the body of a crucified man—and the head of a jackass!

Although this mocking picture offends our Christian sensitivi-

ties, such an artistic travesty would hold no shock for the writers
of the Bible; they knew the cross as an emblem of shame. Look at
some of the terms they used.

They are crucifying the Son of God all over again and subjecting
him to public disgrace. (Hebrews 6:6)

Jesus, the author and perfecter of our faith, . . . endured the
cross, scorning its shame. (Hebrews 12:2)

If you are reproached for the name of Christ, blessed are you,
for the Spirit of glory and of God rests upon you. On their part
He is blasphemed, but on your part He is glorified. (1 Peter 4:14
NKJV)

Christ redeemed us from the curse of the law by becoming a
curse for us, for it is written: "Cursed is everyone who is hung
on a tree." (Galatians 3:13)

The message of the cross is foolishness to those who are
perishing. . . . We preach Christ crucified: a stumbling block to
Jews and foolishness to Gentiles. (1 Corinthians 1:18, 23)

Public disgrace. Shame. Reproach. Blasphemy. Foolishness. Stumbling block. Curse. These are the words Bible writers associated
with crucifixion.

The Pagan View of Crucifixion

Crucifixion was a form of execution reserved for runaway slaves,
rebels, child molesters, thieves who knocked down old ladies,
abusers of their parents—the lowest criminal scum. The Roman
senator Marcus Tullius Cicero, a pagan, wrote, "Let even the name
'cross' be kept away not only from the bodies of the citizens of Rome
but also from their thought, sight and hearing. . . . It is a grave
offense even to bind a Roman citizen, a crime to flog him, almost
the act of parricide to put him to death: What shall I then call
crucifying him? Language worthy of such an enormity—it is im-
possible to find!"

Is it any wonder that the pagan soldier associated crucifixion with repugnance and ridicule and so drew his picture of Christ on the cross with the head of an ass?

Pagans often made such an association. Tertullian mentions another such picture of the God of the Christians. This one shows another man with an ass's head; he wears a toga and carries a book. Minucius Felix said, "Audio eos turpissiame pecudis caput asini . . . venerari"—"I hear they worship the very filthiest beast with the head of an ass." The pagan word for the earliest Christians was *asinarii,* which can be politely translated to mean "belonging to an ass."

Everyone—Hebrew, Christian and pagan—knew that crucifixion was a filthy, disgusting, ignominious way to die. And so the man who mocked Alexamenos drew a picture of him praying to Christ crucified.

Jesus' Own View of His Crucifixion
Jesus himself linked the cross with utter degradation. "Jesus took the Twelve aside and told them, 'We are going up to Jerusalem, and everything that is written by the prophets about the Son of Man will be fulfilled. He will be handed over to the Gentiles. They will mock him, insult him, spit on him, flog him and kill him. On the third day he will rise again" (Luke 18:31-33).

Handed over. Mocked. Insulted. Spat on. Flogged. Crucified.

Yes, Jesus knew what he was getting into, as he explained on the Mount of Transfiguration:

"The Son of Man must suffer many things and be rejected by the elders, chief priests and teachers of the law, and he must be killed and on the third day be raised to life." Then he said to them all: "If anyone would come after me, he must deny himself and take up his cross daily and follow me. For whoever wants to save his life will lose it, but whoever loses his life for me will save it. What good is it for a man to gain the whole world, and yet lose or forfeit his very self? If anyone is ashamed of me and my words, the Son of Man will be ashamed of him when he comes in his glory." (Luke 9:21-26)

Suffer. Tortured. Rejected. Shamed.

Who was Jesus to take such abuse? And why? Why, knowing what lay ahead, did he deliberately go to Jerusalem and crucifixion?

Who Was This Who Was Crucified?

"In the past God spoke to our forefathers through the prophets at many times and in various ways, but in these last days he has spoken to us by his Son, whom he appointed heir of all things, and through whom he made the universe. The Son is the radiance of God's glory and the exact representation of his being, sustaining all things by his powerful word" (Hebrews 1:1-3). And, Paul says, "in Christ all the fullness of the Deity lives in bodily form" (Colossians 2:9).

The owner of all things. The Creator of the universe. The shine of God's glory. The exact replica of God. The sustainer of all things. The fullness of the Deity. That's what the Scripture says about Jesus.

Again and again Jesus alluded to himself not only as the Son of Man but also in terms of God come to earth. He said, "I am the light of the world"; "I am the door"; "I am the bread of life"; "I am the Good Shepherd"; "I am the resurrection and the life." He said that he personally saw Satan fall from heaven before earth's creation. He said he existed before Abraham. He said he could exercise the authority to forgive sin. He said he was Lord of the sabbath. He said that he and the Father are one and the same Person—the Ancient of Days. The Lord of Hosts. The Prince of Peace. Wonderful Counselor. King of kings and Lord of lords. Light of lights. Very God of Very God, begotten not made . . .

The night before Jesus was crucified, Caiaphas, the high priest, asked him, "I charge you under oath by the living God: Tell us if you are the Christ, the Son of God."

"Yes, it is as you say," Jesus replied. "But I say to all of you: In the future you will see the Son of Man sitting at the right hand of the Mighty One and coming on the clouds of heaven." (Matthew 26:63-64)

And Jesus' actions backed up everything he said about himself. He acted like God.

He behaved as we'd expect God to behave—not only on special occasions, such as in the grand finale of his resurrection, when he returned to life, but every day he lived. Jesus walked on water. Jesus calmed a storm. Jesus withered a fig tree. Jesus gave sight to the blind and hearing to the deaf. He fed the hungry, cured the sick, taught the ignorant, confused the proud—whatever was wrong, Jesus made it right.

How else would we expect God to act?

And Who Are We?

One of us betrayed Jesus. One of us smashed a thorny crown on his head. One of us whipped him. One of us whacked him on the head with a stick. One of us stripped him naked. One of us held his arm down while another hammered a nail through his hand. We crucified him.

And then, while he hung on the cross in agony, we mocked him.

"So! You who are going to destroy the temple and rebuild it in three days, come down from the cross and save yourself!" one said.

"He 'saved' others but he can't save himself," another said.

"Let's see if Elijah comes to take him down," called one.

"If you are the Christ, come down now—we'll believe when we see *that*," said another.

"If you are the Son of God, come down from the cross!" shouted another.

"If you are the King of the Jews, save yourself," mocked one.

The mockers demanded that Jesus, if he was indeed God on the cross, do something. And how did Jesus respond? He forgave them.

"Father, forgive them for they don't know what they're doing," he said.

Why the Cross?

Why did the Lord of the universe suffer all this mockery, this humiliation, this shameful treatment? If Jesus really was the Lord God Almighty come in the flesh, and if he really had the power to call legions of angels to his rescue, why did he stay on the cross? He'd have to be crazy to put up with all this if he didn't have to.

That's right!

God is crazy about us. He endured the cross for love of you and me. "You see, at just the right time, when we were still powerless, Christ died for the ungodly. . . . God demonstrates his own love for us in this: While we were still sinners, Christ died for us" (Romans 5:6-8).

The God we pray to, the High and Holy One who inhabits eternity, who dwells among the cherubim, who has heaven as his throne and the earth as his footstool, who holds the entire universe, small as a hazelnut, in the hollow of his hand (as St. Julian of Norwich envisioned)—Jesus somehow lowered himself, emptied himself, reduced himself to enter the world he had created:

He, who had always been God by nature, did not cling to his prerogatives as God's equal, but stripped himself of all privilege by consenting to be a slave by nature and being born as mortal man. And having become man, he humbled himself by living a life of utter obedience, even to the extent of dying, and the death he died was the death of a common criminal. (Philippians 2:5-8 Phillips)

In the early days of computer technology, the machinery for a mainframe filled a whole room in a building; then came the microprocessors, with microchips so small that the same power can now be found in a laptop. Well, God's love motivated him to "microprocess" himself, condense himself down so he could squeeze into this world to get to where the problem was—that's us.

In his essay "The Grand Miracle" C. S. Lewis uses the analogy of a diver to illustrate God's entering the world to save sinners— what theologians call the incarnation:

> One has the picture of a diver, stripping off garment after garment, making himself naked, then flashing for a moment in the air, and then down through the green, and warm, and sunlit water into the pitch black, cold freezing water, down into the mud and slime, then up again in the green and warm and sunlit water, and then at last out into the sunshine, holding in his hand the dripping thing he went down to get.

Down, down, down to the very bottom to get us—that's the incarnation; then up, up, up, back to where he came from—that's the resurrection!

All the degradation, filth and mockery we subjected him to—like unruly, spoiled, vicious brats pounding on a sofa cushion—hardly left a dent, except the nail prints in his hands.

You see, God has no shame.

For love, there's virtually nothing he won't do. He wants princes and princesses for his kingdom, and he'll go to any lengths to get them.

The God Who Would Kiss Frogs

The least intelligent man I ever met was a Christian—just like me.

Jerry cleaned animal cages for a rinky-dink circus that made the rounds of shopping centers years ago. He concentrated on his work to get it just right. He beamed when he talked about his job. He felt proud because the boss trusted him to hose down the tiger cage. He liked to be called Tigerman.

This thirty-two-year-old retarded worker prayed about his job. He held essentially the same religious beliefs I do.

One day I asked Jerry why he was a Christian.

Screwing up his brow in intense deliberation, he painfully tried to remember a Bible verse someone had taught him: "For God so loved the world that he . . . that he . . . That he did something or the other!" Jerry said, grinning.

The smartest woman I've ever met was also a Christian.

Joyce, who had an astronomically high IQ, had earned her doctorate while still a teenager. She spoke fluently in dozens of foreign languages and translated documents for the United Nations.

When I asked her about why she was a Christian, she replied without hesitation, "The love of God." And she quoted the same Bible verse as Jerry: "For God so loved the world that he gave his one and only Son, that whoever believes in him shall not perish but have everlasting life" (John 3:16).

God reached into the world to save people not on the basis of how smart we are, or how good-looking we are, or how rich we are, or how strong we are. Few are smart, few beautiful, few rich, few strong; he loves us all, and saves us all on the basis of his love.

It's not because we are lovable—there's not a single teddy bear in the lot of us.

God's Kink

God loves because it's his own nature to love.

I once knew a man in Kansas who collected paper matchbook covers. I've seen him pick up a matchbook cover straight out of the gutter and treasure it. Now, empty matchbook covers have no intrinsic value—except to the person who values them because of some personal kink.

God has that same sort of kink concerning people. He'll stoop to pick up one that you or I wouldn't even notice. He'll dig through the world's trash to get one of us and brush us off and display us in his collection as a treasure. "How great is the love the Father has lavished on us, that we should be called children of God!" (1 John 3:1).

The cross demonstrates how God lavishes his love on each one of us—but his love does not stop at the cross. Jesus rose from being dead, but his love did not end with his resurrection. Forty days later, Jesus went back to where he had come from originally, but his love did not stop with his ascension.

Where did this path of love—down to mockery, torture and death, up again to heaven—lead him?

To prayer for us.

"He is able to save completely those who come to God through him, because he always lives to intercede for them" (Hebrews 7:25). Right now Jesus is interceding for us. He prays for us. He links his prayers with the prayers that you and I offer. He joins us when we pray.

He has paid dearly in order to do this. He paid the price of love.

So when your prayers are not answered to your immediate satisfaction, and you feel hurt and confused and can't understand what's happening . . .

Know that God loves you.

Why else all that humiliation, all that anguish, all that mockery?

Why else the cross?

— eight —

What Have I Done That's So Awful?

If God knows what I did that day,

will he answer

even one of my prayers?

I THINK THE MOST BEAUTIFUL ROOM IN THE WORLD IS THE MAIN reading room at the Library of Congress in Washington, D.C. I had the privilege of working and studying in that room for several years.

A massive copper dome rises above the Reading Room, supported by tiers of tall, rose-colored marble columns. Regal statues of the Greek Muses stand atop these columns, and between them are huge scrolls lettered with quotations from the world's greatest literature. One of these scrolls contains the words of the prophet Micah:

> Wherewith shall I come before the LORD, and bow myself before the high God? shall I come before him with burnt offerings, with calves of a year old? Will the LORD be pleased with thousands of rams, or with ten thousands of rivers of oil? shall I give my firstborn for my transgression, the fruit of my body for the sin

of my soul? He hath shewed thee, O man, what is good; and what doth the LORD require of thee, but to do justly, and to love mercy, and to walk humbly with thy God? (Micah 6:6-8 KJV)

In a way, Micah's four questions and his answer make everything about living seem relaxed and smooth. But if God really is that easy to satisfy, why do I so often feel terribly ill at ease and guilty when I pray?

I do. I really do.

Sometimes I feel as though I'd borrowed ten dollars from God three weeks ago and had promised to pay him back Friday, but didn't. I avoid him and hope he doesn't notice.

Why do I feel that way? I've never been a gang member or a drug dealer or something awful. All things considered, I'm a pretty nice guy. Okay, so I have stolen a few things, and I have lied a bit, and I have cheated, and then there was that little incident in Denver when—well, you don't need to know about that. But those sins were exceptions to the way I usually behave—weren't they? I can live with those things.

Of course there have been one or two other things that I really feel bad about. I'm not going to tell you the specifics, but once in a while I've done something that disappoints me. I think better of myself than to do a squalid bit of nastiness like that. Really! What kind of guy would do a thing like that? That's disgusting. Rotten. That's not like me at all. I mean, there was no profit in it, I didn't enjoy it, I'd be ashamed and couldn't even explain why I did it if anybody ever found out—but I did it anyhow. And I didn't realize how yucky it was till afterwards—well, yes, there was just a second there, right in the middle of things, when I suppose I could have not . . . but . . . you know what I mean, don't you?

And I'll tell you the truth, a lot of times I worry that the reason my prayers are not answered is that I've done something so awful that God himself will not listen to me. Have you ever thought the same thing yourself secretly?

Our Worry Is Nonsense!

It's pure baloney. What sin could we possibly commit that's bigger than God's love? What could we possibly do that would surprise God?

Let's not exaggerate our importance. We're petty sinners at best. God's Word says: "The blood of Jesus, his Son, purifies us from all sin!"

How much sin?

All.

If we are Christians, then we have the assurance that *all* our sins—past, present and future—are forgiven, covered by the blood of Christ, paid for, removed, gone, kaput.

The old saw defines *justified* as Just As If I'd Never Sinned. God does nothing by halves; when he forgives a sin, that sucker's gone. "As far as the east is from the west, so far has he removed our transgressions from us" (Psalm 103:12).

Could the Bible be lying when it says that?

Not a chance. The King of Glory clothes his followers in righteousness. He "is able to keep you from falling and to present you before his glorious presence without fault and with great joy" (Jude 24). When God forgives you, you're so clean you squeak.

> Who shall separate us from the love of Christ? Shall trouble or hardship or persecution or famine or nakedness or danger or sword? . . . I am convinced that neither death nor life, neither angels nor demons, neither the present nor the future, nor any powers, neither height nor depth, nor anything else in all creation, will be able to separate us from the love of God that is in Christ Jesus our Lord. (Romans 8:35, 38-39)

Dueling Prophets

Now wait a minute here! Doesn't the Scripture teach that sin separates from God, that sin short-circuits prayer, that God does not even hear the cry of the sinner?

Forget Micah's pretty poetry. What about the prophet who said, "Surely the arm of the LORD is not too short to save, nor his ear too dull to hear. But your iniquities have separated you from your God; your sins have hidden his face from you, so that he will not hear" (Isaiah 59:1-2)?

That prophet says our sins shout so loud they drown out our whispered prayers. He declares, "All of us have become like one who is unclean, and all our righteous acts are like filthy rags" (Isaiah 64:6).

What are all these prophets trying to pull? On one hand we read "as far as east is from the west," and on the other hand we read "our righteous acts are as filthy rags." Is the teaching of Scripture contradicting itself?

Not at all. What we have here are two different kinds of sin: sin that has been forgiven and sin that has not been forgiven.

Actually, it's *hard* to go to hell. If a person does manage to go to hell it's only because he or she has fought Almighty God tooth and nail every step of the way. You have to work hard to go to hell. You have to exercise a powerful lot of will and determination to keep God from saving you.

Hey, that's what a Savior does. And Jesus is mighty good at his chosen job.

Yes, he did say, "Wide is the gate and broad is the road that leads to destruction, and many enter through it" (Matthew 7:13). We are a rebellious race, and the Spirit of God will not strive with a person forever. There does come a point when he allows people to go the way they have chosen.

But Jesus seems to consider even the one sheep who goes astray as too many to lose. And heaven is a mob scene! In his vision of heaven, St. John said,

> I looked and heard the voice of many angels, numbering thousands upon thousands, and ten thousand times ten thousand. They encircled the throne. . . . After this I looked and there before

me was a great multitude that no one could count, from every
nation, tribe, people and language, standing before the throne
and in front of the Lamb. . . . And they cried out in a loud voice:
"Salvation belongs to our God,
who sits on the throne,
and to the Lamb." (Revelation 5:11; 7:9-10)
Jesus spoke of multitudes pouring in from the east and west and
north and south to sit at his table. There is room for everyone in
the kingdom of God. No one who wants to be there is turned away.
"Whoever comes to me I will never drive away," Jesus said (John
6:37).

Many on the road to destruction: multitudes rejoicing before the
throne—is *this* a contradiction in Scripture?

Not at all. What we have pictured are *forgiven* and *unforgiven*
people.

So what does all that have to do with our prayers being answered? Bear with me as I circle around the question a bit. We will
end up addressing the issue, I promise.

Of Voting, Algebra, Swimming and Salvation

One hundred percent of the people born in my state, Florida, are
by birthright citizens of the United States; but only 56 percent of
all Floridians are registered voters, and only a small percent of
them actually cast votes in any given election. Thus while everyone
potentially has a voice in our government, few actually exercise
that privilege at the polls.

As a parallel, everyone born into the world is a child of God by
creation, but only a relative few speak out in prayer. In fact, a good
many people choose not to even register in God's kingdom. If that
is their choice, how can they expect to be heard when they do pray?

Now, here is as good a place as any to think about being
saved—it's sort of like registering to vote, getting your name in the
book of life so your voice is heard in heaven.

Let me switch my analogy from voting to mathematics. St. Paul explained salvation to the Christians living at Ephesus in a statement which I think resembles an algebraic equation: "For it is by grace you have been saved, through faith—and this not from yourselves, it is the gift of God—not by works" (Ephesians 2:8-9).

When we remember the axiom "Things equal to the same thing are equal to each other," the equation looks like this:

$$G + F = S = gi$$
$$S \neq Y$$
$$S \neq W$$

Grace + Faith = Salvation = Gift ≠ Yourself ≠ Works.

Grace plus faith equals salvation, which equals a gift of God; salvation does not equal anything from yourself, and it does not equal your works.

Being saved does equal a gift; that gift is equal to faith and grace. God gives you grace. God gives you salvation. God gives the gift.

And what's your part in being saved? Stop fighting God. Let Christ save you. Receive his salvation.

Now for another analogy. Having used voting and math, I turn to swimming in the ocean.

Some of us are like swimmers caught by the undertow, out of breath, panicked, struggling to stay afloat, thrashing about. When the lifeguard comes we fight, biting, pulling hair, battling for all we're worth. We refuse to relax and let the guard (who is, of course, God) tow us to shore.

Others of us are like swimmers who have gone to sleep floating on an air mattress, drifting farther and farther from shore, lulled by the waves and gentle current. When the Savior swims out to save us, we look at him like he's crazy. We tell him, "Go away. I'm all right. I'm doing fine. I don't need any saving. I don't need you." And all the while, Jaws circles out of sight beneath the surface, lurking in wait, ready to bite.

To go to hell, to go on being unsaved and unforgiven, means

resisting God with all your puny power, ignoring the One who demands attention.

To be saved, we need only stop fighting and agree to let him save us.

And agreeing with God and letting him save us brings us back to the relationship between sin and unanswered prayers.

Confession and Prayer

Theology defines *confession* as "agreeing with God about sin." Agreeing with God brings us salvation; agreeing with God is confession; agreeing with God is the way to keep sin from hindering our prayers.

You see, in prayer we can't fake God out. He does know our every need; but that's not all he knows. He also knows our every secret sin.

It is ludicrous to bop in before the throne of God pretending we're his equals—or better. To come before him pretending our own righteousness is to come into the divine court bearing what Isaiah discreetly calls "a menstrual cloth" as our banner before us (Isaiah 30:22).

We have no righteousness—not even a little bit! And we can't fool God into thinking we have.

The secret of forgiven sin is confessed sin; that simply means agreeing with God about our sin. "If we confess our sins, he is faithful and just and will forgive us our sins and purify us from all unrighteousness" (1 John 1:9).

How about that? No matter what we have done or have not done, God zaps that sin clean. He makes us clean. He gives us the purity of Jesus Christ.

Which Sins Should I Confess?

That's a question to ask no one but God. Ask him in your prayers what you should confess, and he will bring certain things to your mind as fast as peaches through a goose.

Don't try to work up guilt feelings and make your own agenda for confessing things. There's a big difference between *confessing* sins and *relishing* them. When I try to psych myself into a confession mode, I find that I begin to mentally rerun and relive certain sins—like enjoying a favorite video again and again. I get positively gleeful about my sin and about what a nice person I am for confessing it. Remember, the heart is deceitful above all things and desperately wicked (Jeremiah 17:9).

However, if I ask God to bring to mind any particular sin I should be confessing at this particular time, he often reminds me of things I haven't thought of for years. Usually they are not the biggies that I still feel proud of, but squalid, petty things that I'll never brag about in the locker room. Agreeing with God, I experience genuine shame that I have offended him and genuine gratitude to him for forgiving me.

I also ask him if I need to confess this sin to any other person. Most of the time I do not need to. But occasionally I do need to go to those I have sinned against, confess to them and ask their forgiveness for being a jerk.

That's humiliating. I hate being humiliated, don't you?

We need to do it anyhow.

Times like that I wish I could just fax in my requests to God without having to bother with him. Sometimes prayer is a pain.

God Doesn't Hold Grudges

But—and this is very, very important—often you will have nothing to confess! That's right. Your sins are forgiven. You're okay. God does not hold grudges.

Confession is agreeing with God, even when he says things are square between the two of you.

Don't try to make out that you're a bigger sinner than you are; that reveals a perverse sort of pride. You are bad enough, but not likely to be in the same class as Hitler. Just be glad that Jesus saves even *petty* sinners.

Ghost Nets

Scuba divers have found that "ghost nets" drift in the ocean. These are sections of monofilament nets which have torn lose from fishing boats. The ghost nets do not dissolve or disintegrate; they never rot away. Instead, they snag on some rusty shipwreck or piling and remain on the ocean bottom for ages.

And they still catch fish! In fact, these loose, cast-off nets capture hundreds of small fish; and larger fish see the little ones in the nets and swim right in, thinking to have an easy meal. But the bigger fish get entangled too. Those entangled fish struggle in the ghost nets till they die.

Every one of us has certain things that lurk like ghost nets down below the surface of our minds. They may be things our parents said, things we did as children, things that embarrassed us, things that shame us, things that make us feel unworthy. They may even be genuine sins that we have confessed but can't let go of in our minds, because we can't forgive ourselves for not living up to our own high expectations.

These mental ghost nets, long ago torn loose from the real situation that generated them, still capture our thoughts. One rotting fish attracts the healthy ones. The enemy of our souls lurks by the ghost nets, whispering, "Look at that. That's the kind of person you are. I'm so disappointed in you. I really expected better. You disgust me."

Recognize his voice? Well, he has been a liar from the beginning.

Don't let any voice tell you that your prayers are not answered because you are unworthy. *Of course* you're unworthy. Nobody ever said you were worthy. Jesus is the one who is worthy. We approach God in his name and none other. It's Jesus or nothing.

But the devil hates to see you pray. He will distract you,

discourage you, deceive you, make you feel guilty when you're not—anything to stifle your prayers.

Ignore him. When you hear his complaints in your ear, refer him to the Management.

When Your Heart Says You're Rotten

When your own heart tells you that you are too sinful, that you have done something too awful, that you are too vile to have God answer your prayers, ignore even your own innermost heart.

That's right! The Scripture says, "For if our heart condemns us, God is greater than our heart, and knows all things" (1 John 3:20 NKJV).

You may not see the answer you expect to every prayer you pray, but if you are a Christian and if you agree with God about whichever of your sins he calls to mind, you can rest assured that God is hearing your prayers.

Forgiven sin does not separate you from God. Your self-condemning heart does not separate you from God.

The blood of Jesus Christ works. It cleanses us from all sin—yes, even that one.

But the relationship between sin and prayer is such a biggie that I think another chapter on the subject is in order.

— nine —

What Am I Doing That's So Awful?

Am I doing something

that keeps God

from answering my prayers?

I USED TO THINK THE RELATIONSHIP BETWEEN SIN AND PRAYER was a sort of bargain with God, saying to him, in effect, "If I do what you want, then you've got to do what I want." In those days I felt that in prayer the deck was stacked against me. I felt God was being unfair. As if he was saying, "Okay, John, if you don't do exactly what I say, then I'm not going to answer your prayers—and it will be all your fault."

That way of thinking views God as a cosmic child who, if we don't play by his rules, will take his ball and go home. This is not the God of the Bible.

The real relationship between sin and prayer is this: *God is not answering our prayer because our underwear is on fire.*

Yep. That's the truth.

We don't see the danger behind us. We hardly feel any heat yet. We're just a trifle uncomfortable, but the God who stands behind us sees the smoke, knows the danger, anticipates the pain and moves to put out the flames before they consume us.

First Things First

We usually pray about the concerns we see, the things we want, the people we love (or who aggravate us), the futures we anticipate, the sins we're worried about. These things—while valid things to pray about—are not necessarily our most immediate and pressing needs.

The second chapter of Mark's Gospel tells how four men brought a paralyzed friend to a house where Jesus was teaching. The crowd that gathered to hear was so dense that they could not get close. They carried their friend up on the roof and dug through the clay, making a hole big enough to lower the paralytic inside, into the room where Jesus was teaching.

What a picture of determined prayer! What unity and agreement these five men displayed. What yearning for healing. What serious faith they demonstrated.

"When Jesus saw their faith, he said to the paralytic, 'Son, your sins are forgiven' " (Mark 2:5).

What? They had not broken through the roof to hear *that!* They expected an answer to their prayers concerning healing.

Can you doubt that they were disappointed?

Mark tells his readers that they eventually did get what they prayed for—but first things came first. God is good at keeping his priorities straight.

While we pray about new clothes, he's concerned about putting out the fire in our pants.

While we pray about whether or not to have cosmetic surgery on our pretty faces, he's dealing with the undetected cancer in our lungs.

His priorities are not ours. He ignores our babble and strives to save tender portions of our anatomy from getting scorched. And we pout and wonder why he does not answer our spoken prayers!

Prayer-Hindering Sins

The Bible says that certain specific things are such a clear, present, immediate and horrible danger to us that God places them *first* on the list of things to be dealt with. Everything else—even our most heartfelt prayers—takes a back seat. If we keep on in these dangerous sins, the Bible tells us our prayers will not work as we might expect otherwise.

What are these things that demand priority in prayer? What looms so large that even our best, our most innocent and what would otherwise be perfectly good prayers are put on hold and hindered?

Husbands, in the same way be considerate as you live with your wives, and treat them with respect as the weaker partner and as heirs with you of the gracious gift of life, so that nothing will hinder your prayers.

Finally, all of you, live in harmony with one another; be sympathetic, love as brothers, be compassionate and humble. Do not repay evil with evil or insult with insult, but with blessing, because to this you were called so that you may inherit a blessing. . . . "For the eyes of the Lord are on the righteous and his ears are attentive to their prayer, but the face of the Lord is against those who do evil." (1 Peter 3:7-9, 12)

That means to get along with people! While these verses at first appear to be addressed specifically to husbands, a complete reading of the passage beginning back at 2:13 reveals that answers to our prayers, whether we are married or not, are related directly to how well we get along with the people closest to us.

You see, while our prayers are concerned with getting certain results and things, God is concerned with making us into a certain kind of person. And no gauge measures what kind of person you are as accurately as the way you treat the people who live closest to you every day. John Wesley, founder of Methodism, once said that when a man becomes a Christian, even his dog knows it!

Peter says to treat your wife with honor and respect as a partner, lest your prayers be hindered. How can you be cozy with God and a slob with your own wife?

Look at the alternative to being the kind of person Peter is talking about: if you are not the kind of guy he describes, you'd be inconsiderate, disrespectful, unsympathetic, proud, vengeful, insulting, petty, unholy, evil—and praying for God to give you a new car!

Hey, we're just doing what comes natural to us. But God calls us to the supernatural.

Be a decent man and husband first, starting today; *then* see how your prayers turn out. And don't snicker, ladies, while he is getting his scriptural licks; each of us, whether husband or wife, must answer to God for how we treat our spouse.

And let's not think that we're home free if we don't happen to be married. There are still people who live close to you whom you must treat decently if your prayers are not to be hindered. How do you treat your roommate, your parents, your little sister?

Oh, but these folks are just family. They take me as I am. When I get home I can kick off my shoes, unwind and be myself.

Exactly! I can be myself with the people closest to me. I can safely disregard some of the common courtesies and manners I have to display to strangers in order to keep my job or make my way in the world. The people I live with bear the brunt of my being myself without restraint.

The flames of hell are fueled with such unrestrained selfdom.

We all have a tendency to treat the people we live closest to as the least important members of our circle, as a base to move up and out from, stepping-stones to more important people and things. Jesus inverts that mental structure. He says "the least of these brothers of mine" are as important as Christ himself. And what makes me think that by "the least" he means someone other than the person I consider least and show the least consideration to?

The least people in my life often speak with the very voice of God. I believe I've heard God's voice in the mouths of my wife and children more often than from any other source. In fact, when my wife says, "John, that's the dumbest thing I've ever heard of," I can almost bet she speaks with divine inspiration.

(Incidentally, when I think I've heard the voice of God through another person, it has always been in some common remark made in general conversation. I'm very leery of the person who comes to me saying the Lord told them to tell me something. I consider such folks kooks, and nothing's ever happened to make me think I was wrong.)

There's another, more practical aspect to how the sin of mistreating those closest to us hinders our own prayers. In my thirty-some years as a Christian, never has some stranger popped up out of nowhere and answered one of my prayers. With virtually every personal prayer that I have seen answered, the human agent instrumental in answering my prayer has been someone close to me!

My wife, my children, my parents, my in-laws, my friends, my church, my neighbors, my associates—these people are the ones God has used to answer the prayers of my heart.

Treat the people closest to you with holiness and awe; sin not against them, lest your actions and attitudes hinder your own prayers.

The Forgiveness Link

Here's another Scripture passage to think about when considering the relationship between our ongoing sins and our prayers.

This, then, is how you should pray:

    "Our Father in heaven,

hallowed be your name,
your kingdom come,
your will be done
   on earth as it is in heaven.
Give us today our daily bread.
Forgive us our debts,
   as we also have forgiven our debtors.
And lead us not into temptation,
   but deliver us from the evil one."

For if you forgive men when they sin against you, your heavenly Father will also forgive you. But if you do not forgive men their sins, your Father will not forgive your sins. (Matthew 6:9-15)

Of all the different elements in the Lord's Prayer, Jesus chose to elaborate on only one: *Forgive me my sins just as I forgive those who sin against me.*

Once I met an elderly woman who raged against her sorry, no-good daughter. "That girl's just street trash," she told me. "She lived with that no-good, drunken lout for two, almost three, years before she got pregnant and they had to get married. She was raised better than that. Mark my words, she'll rue the day she took up with that no-account bum. Never worked an honest day's work in his life. The shameless hussy, I raised her better than for that sort of carrying on . . ."

Later that same day, I meet the Shameless Hussy and her No-Account Husband for the first time; the couple had been married for forty-two years! For decades, bitterness, disappointment and pride had festered inside the mother, souring her spirit.

Surely you've seen this dynamic at work yourself: the student who still complains about what the professor did last semester, the professor who is bitter about the other professor, the retired man who seethes over what management did years ago, the young woman who resents her parents' divorce. Just about everyone you meet, including the person you see in the mirror each morning, falls prey to an unforgiving spirit.

An unforgiving spirit is one of the few things Jesus said could be a cause for unanswered prayer. This is the straightest path to spiritual death.

Grow Ripe or Rot

We either mature or we rot. It's just a matter of time.

You see, as we age we become more and more of what we already are. We move closer to God, or we move further away from him each day. The person who refuses to forgive the wrongs committed by others, who holds on to the hurt, who relishes the resentment, who lets the bitterness curdle inside, sours. Look in any retirement home to see what a grouch such a person becomes in only seventy or eighty years.

On the other hand, the person who forgives the wrongs suffered at the hands of others always mellows and sweetens as the years progress. Have you ever had the pleasure of meeting such a delightful old saint? And think, they got that way in only seventy or eighty years too.

Now think of this: you will live somewhere for all eternity. If you let an unforgiving spirit sour you, what will you be like thirty years from now? Three hundred years from now? Three thousand?

If you forgive, you can sweeten for the next thirty years. For the next three hundred. Eternity will see you glow with the grace of God.

Thoughts on Forgiveness

I have three suggestions about forgiving others in prayer.

First, realize that the wrong they have done you is real. They really did sin against you. The professor really did you dirt. The salesperson really cheated you. The rake really did seduce you and leave. The boss really did discriminate against you. So do not attempt to minimize the sin when you tell God about it. Who knows betrayal better than Jesus? Don't lie to him about your outrage in order to appear cultured and refined—nice—in his sight.

Second, realize that while your feelings on the matter are perfectly valid, forgiveness is not a feeling. It is an act of your will. Therefore, when you pray, do not try to feel good about the people who sinned against you. Believe it or not, those folks are worse than you think! They have done this to you, they have done the same thing to other people, they are likely to keep on doing it again and again! Read the psalmist's imprecatory prayers, such as Psalm 137 (blessings on the man who bashes a Babylonian baby's head against a rock), to see how sentimental *he* felt about Babylonians.

The third thing to realize is that you and I ourselves have done to someone else the same kind of thing that we resent so earnestly. We have caused the same kind of pain that we feel. We have broken someone else's hearts and dreams. We have cheated. We have belittled. We have cheapened. We have stolen. We have betrayed. We have manipulated. We have let others down. We have disappointed. We have lied to. We have dampened joy. We have made someone's life harder than it needs to be. We have sinned.

And we are just as dense about it: we justify it, we excuse it just as the person who has offended us does!

And we do it again and again.

Somebody out there—probably several somebodies—either holds a legitimate grudge or struggles to forgive you and me just as hard as we struggle to forgive those who have trespassed against us.

I am the Babylonian in someone else's prayers!

But I don't feel like a Babylonian.

Nobody does. Even the Babylonians didn't feel like Babylonians. If you were to ask one, he'd say he was just an average guy, maybe a little bit superior to, but anyway as good as, anybody else.

And he's right; he is, you and I are, just about as good as anybody else. And that's not very good.

Be honest with God. Pray and tell him that so-and-so has hurt you, that so-and-so is a modern-day Babylonian, that you have been injured, that you feel outrage; then, as an act of will, deliberately forgive so-and-so. Pray for good things to happen to so-and-so. Then do it again and again, as often as it comes to your attention.

Jesus said, "Love your enemies and pray for those who persecute you, that you may be sons of your Father in heaven" (Matthew 5:44-45).

Ask to be forgiven for your sins just as you forgive so-and-so, because you are at the roots just like so-and-so, only your victims are different.

Prayers get nowhere without forgiveness. It's obvious why, isn't it?

Giving and Getting

So making life harder than it needs to be for people we live with hinders our prayers. And not forgiving people who have sinned against us stifles our prayers. But the Bible teaches that there is another ongoing sin that will flatten our prayers like a frog on the highway. Jesus said, "Do not judge, and you will not be judged. Do not condemn, and you will not be condemned. Forgive, and you will be forgiven. Give, and it will be given to you. A good measure, pressed down, shaken together and running over, will be poured into your lap. For with the measure you use, it will be measured to you" (Luke 6:37-38).

This Scripture passage links the words *forgive* and *give,* the concepts of forgiving and generosity. A lack of generosity is a sin that hinders our prayers.

Does it make sense to expect God to be generous in answering our needs while we act stingy about the needs we see around us? We must help others if we expect God to help us. We need to meet the needs of the needy!

But aren't the poor and homeless just useless winos and bums? Literary agent Curtis Lundgren tells me that according to an Orthodox legend, seven golden, flaming angels walk invisibly in front of every human being, scattering flowers, carrying banners, blowing trumpets and crying, "Make way! Make way for the Image of God!"

If I have anything of this world's goods and see someone in need and I close my heart and do not help that person, then what makes me think the love of God abides with me? (See 1 John 3:17-18.) I dare not ask God Almighty to help me when I refuse to help others. Such prayers are an abomination!

We determine the measure with which our own prayers are answered. So for God's sake—and your own—be magnanimous in giving. Feed the hungry from your own table. When you plan a special meal, bring home a hungry hitchhiker. That guy in rags ought to be wearing your other shirt.

Shelter the homeless. Clothe the naked. Visit the imprisoned. Care for the sick. Comfort the feeble-minded. Spend time with the elderly. Play with the children. Write your mother. Feed the dog. Teach the illiterate to read. Listen to a pest. Tutor the slow. Give blood. Bestow dignity. Do justice. Love mercy. Walk humbly with God.

Good heavens! It looks as if I've stopped thinking with you and started to preach at you—please practice a little of that forgiveness we were just thinking about. Whenever I'm "discussing" something with Jennifer, my oldest daughter, and I drift into a preaching mode, she will listen patiently till I get to a pause and then she'll assume a deadpan expression and recite, "For a tape of today's message, send $19.95 to Box . . ." That always breaks me up, but I hate for her to have to do it. So I'll try to be careful in future chapters.

Anyhow, for heaven's sake, and your own, live Christian. In such a life you forge the measure God uses in answering your prayers.

But wait one minute here. This stuff is plain old good works.

Salvation comes by faith, and it's the prayer of faith that is efficacious. Right?

Right.

But don't forget what King David said about "trust and do":

Trust in the LORD and do good;

dwell in the land and enjoy safe pasture.

Delight yourself in the LORD

and he will give you the desires of your heart. (Psalm 37:3-4)

You see, what we grandiosely call the "ship of life" is in reality a rowboat, and it takes two oars to move the boat on a straight course. Works are an oar, faith is an oar. A person with only one oar in the water splashes around in crazy, erratic circles.

In the next chapter, let's think about the oar called faith and its relationship to answered prayers.

— ten —

Mountain, Get out of My Way: I've Got Faith—Sort Of

If I don't have

a whole lot of faith,

will God answer me?

O NCE UPON A TIME THERE WAS A MAN WHO DECIDED TO TEST
the power of prayer. He had read Matthew 17:20, where
Jesus said, "If you have faith as small as a mustard seed, you can
say to this mountain, 'Move from here to there' and it will move."

Now a mountain just happened to be visible from the man's back
yard, and he decided to make it move by prayer. He picked a night
for the feat and prayed all night long. He bore down and strained
till his face turned red as he prayed. He shouted and screamed and
agonized. He wrestled. He visualized the mountain as already
moved. He reminded God of the verse in Matthew. He thanked God
in advance for the feat. He exerted himself. He urged God. He
wheedled God. He commanded the mountain to move.

Morning dawned. The exhausted man stumbled into his back yard to see if the mountain really had moved. A wonder lay before his eyes!

The mountain still stood where it always had—but miraculously, there in the back yard was a brand-new wheelbarrow and a shovel!

Much as we'd like to believe otherwise, while God does sometimes perform miracles, he does not do tricks. I used to think that if only I had faith, if only I could bear down and believe hard enough, then God had to do what I wanted.

Nonsense. I can't control God.

Faith is something different from that childish attempt at magic; even strong faith does not allow people to control and manipulate God. He is not our sheep; we are his.

What Is Faith?

The Bible defines faith as the substance of things hoped for, the evidence of things not seen (see Hebrews 11:1).

Faith is the substance of hope: it is what hope is made of, hope's material, hope's reality.

Do we ever need hope! A sign in the copier room at the University of North Florida announces:

> **DUE TO CURRENT FINANCIAL CONDITIONS
> THE LIGHT AT THE END OF THE TUNNEL
> WILL REMAIN TURNED OFF TILL FURTHER NOTICE.**

Faith gives hope.

Faith is also evidence. In a trial, evidence is anything that furnishes proof about something that the jury has not seen in person. We know Joe handled the gun because even though nobody saw him, he left the evidence of his fingerprints.

We have solid hope when we see God's fingerprints on a matter.

As the New International Version translates Hebrews 11:1, "Now faith is being sure of what we hope for and certain of what we do not see." This is a far cry from trying to make ourselves believe something that we doubt—that's not faith but wishful thinking. You may not have moved a single mountain this week (has anyone ever?), but you do have more real faith than you think you do.

The Bible on Faith and Prayer

Keep in mind that faith is evidence for hope's substance as we look at some Scriptures that relate faith and prayer.

The morning after Jesus withered a barren fig tree, he told his disciples, "I tell you the truth, if you have faith and do not doubt, not only can you do what was done to the fig tree, but also you can say to this mountain, 'Go, throw yourself into the sea,' and it will be done. If you believe, you will receive whatever you ask for in prayer" (Matthew 21:21-22).

Mark elaborates on this teaching in his Gospel:

Have faith in God. . . . I tell you the truth, if anyone says to this mountain, 'Go, throw yourself into the sea,' and does not doubt in his heart but believes that what he says will happen, it will be done for him. Therefore I tell you, whatever you ask for in prayer, believe that you have received it, and it will be yours. And when you stand praying, if you hold anything against anyone, forgive him, so that your Father in heaven may forgive you your sins. (Mark 11:22-26)

Sometimes I wonder if the apostle James did not have my prayer life in mind when he said, "If any of you lacks wisdom, he should ask God, who gives generously to all without finding fault, and it will be given to him. But when he asks, he must believe and not doubt, because he who doubts is like a wave of the sea, blown and tossed by the wind. That man should not think he will receive anything from the Lord; he is a double-minded man, unstable in all he does" (James 1:5-8).

The link between faith and prayer runs all through the New Testament, but the one that I, as the father of six children, can identify with most personally occurs in Edward Vernon's translation of the Gospel of Mark. At the foot of the Mount of Transfiguration, a man who's worried sick comes to Jesus and says:

"Sir, it is my boy here. I was bringing him to you. Some evil spirit is making him dumb. When it attacks him, it seizes him and throws him to the ground; and his teeth grind together and his lips become covered with foam. His whole body becomes stiff and lifeless. I asked your men to drive out the evil spirit, but they could do nothing."

"What a people you are!" said Jesus. "Always more ready to believe evil things than in the Loving God. How long shall I have to be with you before you believe in God? How long shall I need to be patient with you? Bring the boy here."

They brought the boy to Him, but as soon as the boy set eyes on Jesus the evil spirit rose in a frenzy within him and threw him on the ground, rolling over and over and foaming at the mouth. Jesus turned to the father. "How long has this been going on?"

"Ever since he was quite small," the father replied. "It even throws him into the fire, or into deep water, as if trying to burn him or drown him. Oh, Sir! If you can do anything for him, take pity on his mother and myself, and help us!"

"If I can do anything for him—do you say? Anything can be done for one who believes in God."

"But I do believe in God, honestly I do," the father cried. "Do something to help me believe still more."

Jesus glanced around him. The crowd was growing larger every minute, so without more delay He spoke sharply to the evil spirit: "You deaf and dumb spirit, it is I who am commanding you. Come out of him at once, and stay out!"

The thing shrieked within the boy; it twisted him and threw him about in one last torture, and then—out it came! . . . The boy lay still and pale as a corpse. Everyone thought that he was dead. "He has died," they whispered. But Jesus, bending down, took his hand and lifted him to his feet and the boy stood up.

When they came to their lodging later in the day, the Twelve asked Jesus privately why they had been so helpless in driving out the evil spirit. Jesus replied, "There is only one way of mastering things like that—and that is the way of prayer." (Mark 9:14-29 Vernon)

Reading that passage always gives me the shivers. One of the biggest fears I have as a father is that someone in my family might get sick when I don't have hospitalization coverage or any resources to help. And one of the biggest fears I have as a Christian is that, while I do believe, I don't believe *enough* when the chips are really down. I worry that I don't see the answers to prayer that I want to see because I don't have enough faith.

The boy at the foot of the hill was in bad shape; his father had already taken him to the top healers in the country, and even in the presence of Jesus the kid was still throwing a fit.

Helpless. That's how this father felt. I can sure identify with him. The poor guy had already done everything he knew of to do. He had no resources left. He wasn't even too sure that Jesus could help.

Faith is the substance of hope—even in the stark reality of our own helplessness. By coming to Jesus with a helpless situation, you are already exercising faith! You would not be praying in the first place if you did not already have faith. But faith does not eliminate all questions.

This father questioned. The guy really wondered what was going on. *Why is this happening to me? Why* my *little boy?*

The distraught man questioned: "If you can do anything, take pity on his mother and myself and help us."

" 'If I can'? said Jesus. "Everything is possible for him who believes."

Immediately the boy's father exclaimed, "I do believe; help me overcome my unbelief!" Boy, I sure can identify with this guy!

Questions Focus Faith

The prayer of faith is not an incantation to control God. Questions and responses show that a conversation between two people is taking place. You don't ask the wall questions—you address questions to a person.

Herein is a key fact concerning prayer: We do not *pray about stuff,* we *pray to a Person!* If you were not exercising faith, you would not be asking questions.

To me it's interesting that the dad in Mark 9 didn't offer God any suggestions on how to handle the situation. That's a temptation I often face; I have a tendency to tell him not only what I think is wrong but also how to fix it. The Lord ignores my advise in a surprising number of instances.

Archbishop Fénelon said, "Can we better glorify God than by renouncing ourselves and our own will and letting Him do according to his good pleasure? . . . To wish to serve Him in one place rather than another, by such and such a way, and not by the opposite one, is to wish to serve Him in our own way, and not in His."

The prayer of tenuous faith in the story of the demonized boy shows us that the dad told God about what he lacked. He did not demand that God act according to his own preconceived solution. This father knew what he wanted, and he knew whom to ask. And he trusted God to work out the how.

Faith relates not to a feeling or an event, but to a Person. You see, faith in prayer is faith in a Person, not in a series of events.

The father and mother in this story did not have any idea how to solve their problem. Helpless, they sought him who is the Help of the Helpless. Not knowing the answers, they questioned the right Person. Confused and unsure of themselves, they turned to the One who is trustworthy.

Faith in prayer is not a feeling you work up about a situation or event; faith in prayer is an expression that you have seen some evidence that there is Someone who gives you hope. Faith is not gritting your teeth to believe something good about a bad situation; faith can well be our tearful smile welcoming Jesus into the midst of our losing battles against overwhelming odds, our blindness, our convulsions. Faith in prayer is not a tool to pry favors out of a reluctant God who is trying to hold off doing good for us as long as possible. Faith does not rest in our request, in our wrestling or even in the result we envision. Faith is always in the Person, not the thing.

Let me say it again: Efficacious faith in prayer always relates to the Person we pray to, not to the things we pray for.

Sounds as if I've gone and started preaching at you again. For a tape of today's message, send $19.95 to . . .

Faith to Move a Minivan

Here's a recent example of how faith "worked"—or didn't work—in prayer for my wife and me.

Like most parents, we spend a lot of time driving kids around to this and that—Scout meetings, piano lessons, concerts, youth meetings, museum classes, bus trips and so forth. In fact, we think a father can be defined as a guy who hangs around dark parking lots at night; I think that like most fathers I have spent half my life in some parking lot waiting for some kid to get out of a class. Anyhow, for years my wife and I have prayed almost daily for a minivan to help with all this driving.

And we believed that God was going to help us get a minivan. We were sure of it. We expected it. We were so confident of this that we drove to a dealer and priced minivans and decided which one we were going to buy. To describe in detail what happened next would be like giving a bubble-by-bubble account of the *Titanic*'s sinking, but in brief . . .

I lost my job. A job prospect for Ginny evaporated. The IRS applied our anticipated tax refund to a previous year's bill. An in-the-pocket book contract failed. An expected check stayed expected. And within weeks our bank-account balance dropped to $1.77.

We ended up with no minivan and no money, and to this day we have no prospects of getting either one.

So what happened to our faith? Oddly enough, nothing.

Yes, we did feel hurt and confused and scared. And we questioned. Why had God led us to believe that we were getting out of our financial hole? Why had he let us feel such solid confidence that we could get that minivan we'd prayed for so long? Why did he let us waste so much time visiting dealers and pricing minivans if he were not going to let us buy one? Those were our questions and doubts on one level.

But on another level, from the very first time we'd prayed for a minivan years ago, our faith was not in a minivan. Our faith was not even that God would give us a minivan. Our faith was in God—raw God. And our faith on that level was not disappointed.

Does what I just said make any sense? Maybe a biblical example will show faith better.

Faith in a Person: God

In the book of Romans, St. Paul emphasizes that Abraham's faith, not Abraham's success in keeping rules, saved him. "Abraham's faith was credited to him as righteousness" (Romans 4:9). God had told Abraham that even though he was about one hundred years old, he would father a baby with Sarah, who was no spring chicken herself. But Paul does not say that Abraham believed he'd get Sarah pregnant (the specific occasion). He says, "Abraham believed God" (Romans 4:3). The person of God was the object of Abraham's faith; the specific occasion was important, yet almost incidental. Later, Paul says that Abraham "is our father in the sight of God, in whom he believed—the God who gives life to the dead and calls things that are not as though they were" (Romans 4:17).

Over and over, the New Testament emphasizes that faith is a gift of God; it is not something we work up of ourselves. St. Paul says, "Faith comes from hearing the message, and the message is heard through the word of Christ" (Romans 10:17).

What message? What word?

Paul explained it at—confusing—length, so let's try to follow his reasoning carefully. Here goes:

Moses describes in this way the righteousness that is by the law: "The man who does these things will live by them." But the righteousness that is by faith says: "Do not say in your heart, 'Who will ascend into heaven?' " (that is, to bring Christ down) "or 'Who will descend into the deep?' " (that is, to bring Christ up from the dead). But what does it say? "The word is near you; it is in your mouth and in your heart," that is, the word of faith we are proclaiming: That if you confess with your mouth, "Jesus is Lord," and believe in your heart that God raised him from the dead, you will be saved. For it is with your heart that you believe and are justified, and it is with your mouth that you confess and are saved. (Romans 10:5-10)

Say what?

I think all that means that Jesus Christ is Lord. He returned from the dead. He lives now and makes intercession for us at the right hand of God.

This is the message.

This is the word of Christ.

Faith comes from hearing that Christ died and rose from death. These facts generate faith.

If, when we pray, we are talking with the Resurrected Christ, the Lord of Life, the Victor over our biggest dilemma, death, then the immediate, specific material thing or problem we are talking with him about (whether a minivan, overwhelming enemies, our own health or even foaming-at-the-mouth convulsions in someone we love), while still very important to us, becomes manageable because Life himself listens to our prayer.

That is the substance of our hope, the evidence for our expectations in prayer.

Our faith is based on nothing less than Jesus' blood and righteousness; he arose. Why else would we pray to him?

I Have Faith—So What?

I believe in the person of Jesus. I believe he is the Creator come to earth, the Son of God who died for our sins and rose from the dead.

I believe the Person—Lord, help my unbelief—but I still have a problem with the specifics. The things I pray about are vital to me. I don't want warm fuzzy faith feelings. I want a minivan. I want concrete answers. I want solutions to my problems. I want answers. These things are necessary to my life.

Or are they?

St. Francis of Assisi once said, "Other than God himself, there is no such thing as a necessity of life."

What did he know? He was a *saint,* for goodness' sake! Saints don't need money, do they? He didn't have kids. He didn't need a minivan. I do.

From the Scriptures, it sure looks to me as though Jesus promised specific answers to specific prayers. So maybe the cause for unanswered prayers lies in some other direction that we haven't thought about yet.

Let's keep looking. I'll bet I know what the problem is. Maybe the reason my prayer is not answered is that somebody else is praying that it won't be.

— eleven —

Conflicting Prayers

If the other guy prays for that

and I pray for this and God answers him,

then do I just lose out?

PERIODICALLY THROUGH HISTORY, UNWASHED, UNCOUTH BAR-barian hordes have swept down out of the bleak, frozen north to overrun, rape, pillage and destroy the home of civilization, culture and refinement in the sunny lands to their south. In China, Genghis Khan's Mongolian rabble pillaged civilization. In Europe, Attila the Hun's marauders plunged the Roman Empire into the Dark Ages. And, of course, in this country Abraham Lincoln's Yankees . . .

Actually, even as an unbiased and totally objective Southerner, I have to admit that Lincoln may have had a few good points. Whatever else he did, he was right about freeing slaves.

In 1862, in the midst of what is known in my state as the War of Northern Aggression, Abraham Lincoln wrestled with a problem concerning prayer. The president realized that devout Christians lived in both the Union and the Confederacy. People on both sides were praying for the safety of their loved ones in battle and for peace. And devout people on both sides prayed for victory.

President Lincoln summed up the problem of such conflicting prayers in this way: "In great contests, each party claims to act in accordance with the will of God. Both may be—but one must be—wrong. God can not be for and against the same thing at the same time!"

Two applicants, or a dozen, praying for one job opening. Two suitors praying for the hand of one young woman. Two football teams praying to win the big game.

God must be for one and against the other. Right?

Maybe.

Oddly enough, the Bible hardly acknowledges the problem that bothered President Lincoln. The closest Scripture comes to touching on this problem, as far as I know, is when Jesus talks about persecution. He told his disciples, "A time is coming when anyone who kills you will think he is offering a service to God" (John 16:2).

Not a particularly comforting thought, is it?

Us and Them at Prayer

In the matter of conflicting prayers, the general tone of Scripture is one of assurance that borders on arrogance. The Bible writers make virtually no allowance for a difference of opinion. In the Old Testament, when the record deals with God's relationship to a particular nation, this is not surprising. Moses prayed for the defeat of the Egyptians in no uncertain terms and saw their defeat. Any Egyptian nationals who desired to follow God left Egypt along with Israel and were assimilated among the Jews.

When Joshua led the conquest of Jericho, God gave orders that every man, woman, child, goat, sheep, ox, cow and horse in the city was to be killed. The only exceptions were Rahab and her family, who were all assimilated into the children of Israel. The prayers of the Canaanites inside Jericho, assuming they did pray, are not even recorded in Scripture.

The Jews prayed as God's children, and outsiders hardly stood a chance to contact God except by becoming Jewish. This is understandable in that the Jews prayed to the one living God, whereas the Gentiles around them prayed to idols. No contest there.

God's People in Prayer Conflict

Internal conflicts among the Jews themselves, however, present a different problem. Sometimes this Jew and that Jew, while both supposedly acting in accordance with God's will, prayed for opposite things. But the record shows that God vindicated the person who was really on his side.

For instance, when Moses came in conflict with another Jew, the other man—or woman, in the case of Miriam—had to give way before the chosen man of God. The earth opened and swallowed Korah. Leprosy claimed Miriam. This pattern runs all through the Old Testament.

In 1 Kings 22 and in 2 Chronicles 18, we read about four hundred "prophets" who urged the kings of Judah and Israel to attack the Syrian army. They prayed for victory in the battle. One of these, the prophet What's-His-Name, made himself a headdress sporting a set of iron horns to demonstrate how the good guys would gore the Syrians. But one lone prophet named Micaiah, son of Imlah, said Syria would defeat the kings of Israel and Judah. "I saw all Israel scattered on the hills like sheep without a shepherd, and the LORD said, 'These people have no master. Let each one go home in peace,' " Micaiah reported (1 Kings 22:17).

The horned prophet slapped Micaiah in the face. The kings decided to follow the advice of the four-hundred-prophet majority. They arrested Micaiah and threw him in jail on a strict diet of bread and water.

Then they marched off to battle. The Syrian army creamed them. Guess what happened to What's-His-Name: the Syrians got him. And his horns.

Now, each one of God's chosen leaders did meet with opposition. These enemies sometimes prevailed; they jailed, persecuted or even killed God's leaders. But the opposition was soon revealed as anti-God. Over and over we read how the person who was really on God's side was set against a false prophet. The prayers of one were answered, the prayers of the other were not.

My point is that in Old Testament times, God's chosen leaders were so marked as his leaders, and God's cause was so marked as God's cause, and God's will was so evidently God's will, that no one could fail to see it for long!

The people who followed Jesus in New Testament times encountered differences among themselves as well. Peter and James viewed the Gentiles differently from the way Paul did (see Galatians 2:11-14). Paul's view prevailed in this matter, but many other factions arose among Christians who were praying to the same God about the same concerns. Many in the church at Corinth, for example, argued about which leader to follow—Paul, Apollos or Peter.

Such differences last to the present day. What should we think about them?

Christ's Unearthly Kingdom

Jesus made it clear: "My kingdom is not of this world" (John 18:36). Today, the kingdom of God on earth, the church universal, is an invisible kingdom. No single Christian denomination or school of theology monopolizes truth. And, though many claim to be, no single earthly spiritual leader is indisputably God's Chosen Leader.

Sad to say, almost daily we see fine Christian leaders of all persuasions ensnared by greed, lust or just plain foolishness. In fact, any Christian you look at long enough is sure to disappoint you. Christians are not Christ.

But the fact is that the woods are full of Christians. Anywhere you go you are likely to find some saint serving cheerfully in some difficult, humble, thankless position. Schools, nursing homes, hospitals, welfare offices, shopping malls, filling stations, skid row missions, resort hotels—almost anytime you move beyond your immediate theological circle, you find devout brothers and sisters from all sorts of Christian traditions.

Even in heaven!

Once a friend of mine, a flaming liberal who calls me a rabid fundamentalist, teased me with this old joke:

A Presbyterian businessman died and went to heaven. He was greeted at the gates by several friends from work who had died before him. There were his Catholic secretary, the Methodist clerk out of the mail room, the Episcopalian janitor, the Baptist vice president—all of them rejoicing to see him home.

The group prepared a great welcoming feast for him, then showed him around, pointing out heavenly landmarks: the Great White Throne, the Tree of Life, the Pearly Gates, the streets of gold, the Crystal Sea.

The group grew quite rowdy, enthusiastically pointing, laughing, shouting and asking him questions to catch up on earth news. But approaching one magnificent marble palace set within a walled garden filled with luscious greenery, blossoming flowers and sparkling fountains, all the group suddenly fell silent. "Shhh," one friend whispered. "Go by on tiptoes and don't make a sound."

"Why?" the Presbyterian asked.

"Brotherly love," the friend whispered.

They all tiptoed past in silence. Once away from the mansion, they resumed talking.

"What was that all about?" asked the Presbyterian. "What did you mean by 'brotherly love'?"

"Well, that mansion is for fundamentalists only, and we always tiptoe past because it might spoil heaven for them if they knew the rest of us were here."

That story certainly doesn't do justice to heaven, but as a fundamentalist Christian myself, I can appreciate the humor, and the sadness, in it.

Heaven is full of people. Jesus said they will flock in from the south and east and west—and yes, there will even be Yankees from the North. The Lord has room for everyone.

And he has room for the prayers of everyone, even when those prayers conflict.

For Instance ...

When my son John entered the military, I prayed for his safety daily, because he worked in a dangerous area. As a Christian with a keen sense of responsibility, John prayed extensively about fulfilling his duties efficiently.

On two different occasions, a number of men in John's charge were killed while he was on duty but working in another place. This caused him great anguish. John told me that he felt enormously guilty and responsible, even disappointed that he had not been killed with the others.

In this case I felt my prayers had been answered; John felt his prayers had not been answered.

It took him a long time to realize that our prayers had not been mutually exclusive. He was doing his duty, and at the same time he was kept safe. God, in fact, had answered prayer for both of us; but John had trouble coming to terms with his feelings about the matter (and his feelings have little to do with the facts of the matter).

Our View, God's View

We all see only our own little world. I see my wife. My children. My job. My plans. My wants. You see these same elements in your little world, and you give the ones close to you the same importance in your prayers as I give to my own. Joe sees his wife, children, job, plans, and he prays for them. That's as it should be. It is fitting and proper that we each pray for the people and concerns within our personal sphere of influence. And God takes all these prayers into consideration as he answers.

In early 1992, after President Bush gave his State of the Union address to Congress, CBS News presented an hour-long survey program in which seven million people called in to a computer in Omaha, Nebraska, to register their opinions on political questions. The computer immediately tabulated all these varied opinions.

A magnificent feat of technology.

Well, God made the brains of the people who made the computer. He can handle *more* than seven million prayers an hour. As the psalm says, "His understanding is infinite" (Psalm 147:5 NKJV).

Once I asked Fred—my oldest son, who was then about seven—about that verse; he'd memorized it for a first-grade Vacation Bible School class. Patiently, as though I were a dolt, he explained, "*Infinite* means that God's got all the jelly you've got bread for."

Out of the mouths of babes, you, God, have perfect praise—among other things.

God is. God is infinite. He is good. He is holy. He is almighty. He is love. He is omniscient. He is omnipresent. And he brings all these attributes to bear for us when we pray.

Paul explains the whole matter in only 187 easy steps.

For this reason I kneel before the Father, from whom his whole family in heaven and on earth derives its name. I pray that out of his glorious riches he may strengthen you with power through his Spirit in your inner being, so that Christ may dwell in your hearts through faith. And I pray that you, being rooted and established in love, may have power, together with all the saints, to grasp how wide and long and high and deep is the love of Christ, and to know this love that surpasses knowledge—that you may be filled to the measure of all the fullness of God.

Now to him who is able to do immeasurably more than all we

ask or imagine, according to his power that is at work within us, to him be glory in the church and in Christ Jesus throughout all generations, for ever and ever! Amen. (Ephesians 3:14-21) Notice how many individual people, living and dead, in all generations Paul's prayer involves. Notice how many of the various attributes of God are mentioned. Notice that more than we can either ask or imagine is included.

And notice that God's purposes are more than we bargain for when we pray. He's interested in stuff like

☐ strengthening me with power in my inner being

☐ Christ dwelling in my heart

☐ rooting and establishing me in love

☐ giving me power to grasp the love of Christ

☐ helping me know love that surpasses knowledge

☐ filling me with his own fullness

Wow!

And here all I was praying for was to beat Joe out in getting that new job.

God does not fool around when we pray. As our loving Father, he's got plans for us.

We Are God's Children

Yes, we are the children of God. Trouble is, we think of ourselves as grown-up sons and daughters, independent and on our own, but humoring the Old Man. I suspect a better translation of the biblical term might be "the two-year-olds of God."

Sometimes I think we are playing one game while God is playing another on the same field. Maybe it's a little like a father's discovering his children playing "house" or "doctor" with the kids next door. The children think they are simply playing an enjoyable game; the dad realizes that his kids are developing lifelong sexual attitudes.

Our Father in heaven realizes that the games we play are much more serious than we ourselves realize. So often the things we pray for are tiny game pieces compared to the wonders God has in store for us.

Take my favorite Bible character, Saul—not the one who writes the long theological sentences; the other one.

Saul's father lost some donkeys. Saul hunted them for a week or so and couldn't find them. He decided to go to the prophet Samuel and consult the Lord. Then God ordered Samuel to anoint Saul as the first king of Israel. And here the only thing poor Saul had been praying for was to find his donkeys!

I think that's typical of all our prayers. We want a dime to go to the corner convenience store for candy, while our Father's trying to get us in the car for a trip to a place better than Disneyland!

Eye has not seen, nor ear heard,

Nor have entered into the heart of man

The things which God has prepared for those who love Him.

(1 Corinthians 2:9 NKJV)

At this point, I'm not surprised if you are thinking, *John hasn't answered the question he raised in the first place about conflicting prayers; he's trying to fob off on us that old cliché "pie in the sky by and by."*

You're right. That's the only pie there is. Anything less is ashes.

As a saint—I think it was Jim Elliot, a missionary speared to death by Auca Indians in Ecuador—once observed, "No one in Heaven will complain about having lacked anything on earth."

Here the Lord God Almighty offers us glory unspeakable, the deepest desire of our hearts, an eternal quality of Life unending. And we sulk because our prayers are not answered exactly as we expect.

Could we be expecting the wrong things when we pray?

— twelve —

What Did You Expect?

*If I pray for this
and instead that comes,
is that an answer to my prayer?*

MY MOTHER WAS AFRAID OF DOCTORS AND HATED TO GO TO them. In fact, *hated* is not a strong enough word.

Once, when she was seriously ill, after she and I had discussed it at length, I drove her to a hospital emergency room. At the entrance, she changed her mind and refused to get out of the car. When I went inside to ask a nurse for help, Mama panicked, jumped out of the car and began running across the parking lot. I ran after her and when I caught up, she began to slap me, scratch my face and beat me with her purse. A hospital security guard saw the ruckus and ran to help the poor, defenseless old lady being attacked by the ugly brute.

Fortunately, the ER nurse arrived on the scene before he shot me. She escorted my mother, all sweetness and light by then, inside to see the doctor.

Mama insisted that I wait in the car. Soon she emerged, saying the doctor had examined her and told her she only had a bad cold. I drove her home.

The following day, a policeman appeared at my door. Since I did not have a telephone, the doctor had asked him to contact me in person to tell me the news: my mother was in immediate danger. Her "bad cold" was a virulent cancer that could kill her at any moment.

So I drove over to her house to discuss her illness with her for at least the fortieth time. I was amazed to find her attitude about accepting medical help had completely changed because of a story she'd heard the night before.

This is the story told to my mother by Sister Mary Kevin, who was then president of the Nurses Christian Fellowship in Jacksonville, Florida.

God Will Save Me

It seems that there was a great flood, and a man took refuge on the top of his house and prayed for God to save him.

Some people came floating by on an uprooted tree. "Grab hold of a branch! It's floating toward shore!" they yelled.

"No. I'm not going to chance it. I'm praying for God to save me," he called back.

Soon two men in a rowboat bumped against the rooftop where the man prayed. "Climb in and we'll row you out," they said.

The man refused to get in the open boat. "God will save me," he said. He spent the night on the rain-swept roof, praying for deliverance.

In the morning, a helicopter swooped in overhead and dangled a rope ladder down to the man. The pilot spoke over the loudspeaker: "Climb up the ladder and we'll fly you to dry land."

The flood victim looked at the swaying ladder and listened to the noise of the beating rotors and remained on his roof. "Go get somebody else!" he yelled. "I'm praying for God to deliver me."

Not long after this, the torrent undermined the foundation of the man's house and swept it away. The praying man drowned.

In heaven, he questioned, "Lord, why didn't you save me when I prayed?"

The Lord answered, "I sent you a floating tree, a rowboat and a helicopter. What more did you expect?"

This story changed Mama's attitude about accepting help. She did allow herself to be treated. The chemotherapy and radiation treatments she had feared so much did ease her pain before her death.

Recognizing Answers to Prayer

I find that I often have the same trouble as that man on the rooftop; sometimes I don't recognize an answer to my prayers even if one bites me on the leg.

I'm not alone.

Joe prayed for money to go to college next semester, yet every month when his Record of the Month Club sent him a catalog, he bought twenty-five or thirty dollars' worth of compact disks. He wondered why God did not answer his prayer for college money.

Could it be that God sent the cash, but Joe blew it?

When God does the unexpected, are we so dense that we refuse to give him credit? We sometimes limit God by building up our expectations for an answer that will come at a certain time and in a certain way. And when it does not come according to our instructions to the Almighty, we think he has not answered us at all.

François Fénelon, author of *Christian Perfection,* said: "As for myself, when I suffer I can see nothing but unlimited suffering before me; and when the time of consolation comes, my natural impulse is to dread accepting it, lest it be a mere delusion, which will make the renewed cross heavier."

Archbishop Fénelon, who was court chaplain to King Louis XIV, once wrote a letter to the king's mistress, Madame de Maintenon, in which he said:

It is most important never to anticipate. One of the weightiest rules of the spiritual life is to abide in the present moment, without looking beyond. . . .

Let us then think only of the present, and not even permit our minds to wander with curiosity into the future. The future is not yet ours; perhaps it never will be. It is exposing ourselves to temptation to anticipate God and to prepare ourselves for things which He may not destine for us. . . . Why should we desire to meet difficulties prematurely, when we have neither strength nor light as yet provided for them? Let us give heed to the present, which is pressing upon us; it is fidelity to the present which prepares us for fidelity in the future.

In other words, God is able to handle this bus without any back-seat driver telling him how fast to go, which way to turn, when to stop or even where to fill up. He knows whether it's best to take the expressway or the scenic route, to cross the bridge or take the tunnel, to barrel straight through the city or go around the beltway. Sit back and relax; he'll get us where we need to be.

God is infinite. He is not limited. He can meet any specific need of his people in a variety of ways.

For instance, the need for food. When Moses led the Israelites out of Egypt, they got hungry in the desert and God sent them manna to eat, bread from heaven falling like dew each morning.

When Samson got hungry, God caused a swarm of bees to build a honeycomb for him inside the dried rib cage of a dead lion.

When David's starving men were escaping from King Saul, David led them to the tabernacle and let them eat the consecrated bread from the altar, and years later Jesus commended him for his common sense in doing so (Mark 2:24-27).

When Elijah the Tishbite hid in the cave, he got hungry and God caused ravens to fly in with bits of bread and meat in their beaks for him to eat.

Pretty impressive answers to prayers for food, aren't they? But get this.

A few years back when my family was hungry and I prayed to the Lord to provide us with something to eat, guess what God sent? Not manna, not lions, not bees, not ravens. He sent me to the United States Department of Agriculture Food Stamp Program.

One Sunday after church, we were sitting down to a sparse lunch of hot dogs when a friend came to visit, bringing his date. We had only enough bread to go with the children's hot dogs, we adults had to split one between us, and we had no mustard or catsup. The young woman my friend had brought to visit us worked as a counselor in the food stamp program, and she urged me to apply for stamps that next week.

I was furious with God.

I had prayed for daily bread, and I expected him to answer with a better job, a cash gift, a flock of ravens—something special. Certainly not food stamps!

As I complained, long and loud, to the Management, a thought entered my mind: *Ravens, indeed! John, just who do you think you are, the president of the Audubon Society? Have you ever knowingly seen a raven in your whole life? Could you tell a raven from a great blue heron if one lit on your shoulder? You prayed for food, and here is a source of food. God has promised to provide for your belly; nowhere does he promise to provide for your vanity!*

You see, I had prayed, but I did not want the answer God sent. As I had prayed for food, I'd also imagined how I'd like it served. I anticipated a pleasant answer, one that would allow me not only to eat, but to eat in the dignified style to which I wanted to become accustomed.

The only way to learn humility is to be humiliated.

Virtually all my adult life I have earned well below the income set by the U.S. government as the poverty level. A tiny bit of my situation came about by deliberate choices I made; some of it was caused by circumstances; much of it came from bad management on my part.

I have worked a number of low-paying jobs to supplement my writing income and allow me time to write. I have dug graves, guided tours, worked out of a day labor pool, raised mosquitoes for test purposes, cleaned up toxic-waste dumps, written obituaries and so on and so on. These endeavors have produced a subsistence, but usually adequate, income.

When I arrived at the food stamp office for my appointment, the counselor (naturally, the one I'd met Sunday worked out of a different office) felt suspicious: perhaps I was a rich guy trying to sneak into the program. She demanded proof of my income. And since that income was so erratic, she required that I report to her office often thereafter with a calendar showing where I had worked, what I'd earned and how I'd spent it.

This requirement galled me. Would I be in that office if my family didn't desperately need the help? Would anyone? But, oddly enough, the rule proved to be a great blessing in helping me recognize answers to my prayers.

I searched the house for a calendar. The only one I could find was a free mail-out from Kellogg's Frosted Flakes cereal. A bright picture of Tony the Tiger decorated each page.

So beneath Tony's smiling face, I began keeping a record of how many hours and where I worked each day and how much I got paid. For months I faced the humiliation of taking Tony in and having a suspicious counselor examine and question every entry. I hated that. *Hated* it!

But God thought it was good for my disposition. I hate to admit it, but it was.

You see, I also used the Tony the Tiger calendar to jot down various things I prayed for each day. Before long, I began to jot down answers to these prayers as I saw them come about. Then I began to draw a red line between each prayer and its answer.

The result amazed me.

Red lines crisscrossed my days. *My prayers were being answered all the time.* But I hadn't realized it before, because I hadn't kept any record.

Now I keep a journal that serves to remind me of God's dealings with me day by day. It reveals that he answers many more prayers than I'd give him credit for otherwise.

Forgotten Prayers

Remember, the heart is deceitful above all things. We pray for something, and it comes to pass and we say, "That's nice; I sort of hoped that would happen."

We tend to forget what we have prayed for, to figure that certain things would have happened anyhow and chalk them up to coincidence. In the midst of daily annoyances, we lose sight of long-term prayers. A single burr in the toe of my sock assumes more importance than a whole field full of flowers. In my mind the present aggravation seems more "real" than all of God's past and present blessings.

When I don't see the good I've prayed for happen immediately, my mind naturally leaps to the conclusion, "Ah-ha, just as I suspected. Prayer does no good." And when good things do happen, I figure they were my natural due—forgetting that I had prayed for this very thing! Either way, I neglect to recognize or give God credit for what he is doing for me right now.

That's why I find keeping a daily record of my prayers and problems is such a help. I can flip back to last month or last year and see God in actions that in the pressure of the immediate I had not recognized.

A constant theme of the psalms is that we should remember and recount God's goodness to us. The psalmists constantly harp on this theme. Psalm 111 is a good example:

Praise the LORD.

I will extol the LORD with all my heart
    in the council of the upright and in the assembly.

Great are the works of the LORD;
   they are pondered by all who delight in them.
Glorious and majestic are his deeds,
   and his righteousness endures forever.
He has caused his wonders to be remembered;
   the LORD is gracious and compassionate.
He provides food for those who fear him;
   he remembers his covenant forever. (vv. 1-5)

Praying for What I Already Have

I find that many times I pray to get things I already have.

Perhaps a spirit of dissatisfaction rules our age. Perhaps plain old greed often motivates me. But I find that I am often discontent with my lot in life and want God to step in and substitute something I consider better. In other words, what I call praying might better be termed "verbalized coveting."

For instance, I pray to own a home, and I get frustrated with God when I can't buy one. What's wrong with the place we rent now? Nothing really, but I want to own one. Did Jesus own a home? No, but I want one.

You see, Lord, Bob and Betty are Christians, and they bought a new home in Mandarin.

What is that to you? Follow me.

But I want security.

What is more secure than walking in God's will?

Nothing. But still I covet things. I own a car, a Cadillac that's twenty years old. It's a perfectly adequate car. It gets me wherever I need to go. But I want a giant raven to swoop in bearing a new car in its beak. A Thunderbird would be nice—er, as a car, that is, not as the messenger bird.

When we find ourselves getting greedy in our prayers, the message we need is not about the gospel promises of answered prayer but John the Baptist's message to soldiers: "Be content with your pay" (Luke 3:14). After all, "godliness with contentment is great gain" (1 Timothy 6:6).

Most of us seldom feel content with what we have. As my grandfather used to say when he heard us kids gripe, "There's some folks who'd complain if you was to hang 'em with a brand-new rope."

And St. Paul warns: "People who want to get rich fall into temptation and a trap and into many foolish and harmful desires that plunge men into ruin and destruction. For the love of money is a root of all kinds of evil. Some people, eager for money, have wandered from the faith and pierced themselves with many griefs" (1 Timothy 6:9-10).

The apostle James made this observation: "What causes fights and quarrels among you? Don't they come from your desires that battle within you? You want something but don't get it. You kill and covet, but you cannot have what you want. You quarrel and fight. You do not have, because you do not ask God. When you ask, you do not receive, because you ask with wrong motives, that you may spend what you get on your pleasures" (James 4:1-3).

The Prayer Behind the Prayer

I sometimes wonder if God doesn't look behind our specific prayer for such-and-such and grant us the underlying desire that motivates us to ask.

Here's an example.

In A.D. 383, a young man named Aurelius ran away from his Christian mother's home in Carthage and sailed to the Sin City of the day, Rome. He intended to get out from under her thumb. "The allurements of Rome drew me thither," he said. "They enticed me to another mode of life, to taste of the earth."

Her son's running away devastated the poor mother. She had faithfully prayed for his conversion for years; now he was plunging headlong into overt sin and degradation. The son later wrote about his mother's anguish on the night he sailed away: "My mother shockingly lamented my departure. . . . She clung wildly to me. . . . The floods of my mother's tears would not be dried from her eyes. . . . She was mad with grief. With complaints and lamentation she filled God's ears."

Why did God ignore this godly woman's urgent prayers that night? In spite of her prayers, her son slipped aboard the ship and sailed.

Everything she feared happened to her son in Rome. He moved in with his girlfriend with no intention of marriage. He fell in with a bad crowd. He was exposed to the racetracks and the gladiatorial games. He said he became "filled full of the most execrable defilements." But something else happened to him in Italy: he met a godly Christian man, Ambrose, who influenced Aurelius Augustinus, the future St. Augustine, to come to Christ and be converted! St. Augustine felt that God had led him to Rome for this very reason. He felt that his voyage to Rome had been the answer to his mother's deepest prayers.

In his *Confessions* he wrote of that night he sailed and she cried: "She begged You, my God, with tears so plentiful, that You would stop my sailing, but deeply planning and hearing afar the real core of her longing, You disregarded the prayer of the moment, in order to make me what she always prayed that I should be. . . . You, God, took no notice of her urgent prayers that night because you were tearing me away by my own desires precisely in order to put an end to those same desires. . . . She did not know what joy You were about to build for her out of my absence. That is why she wept and wailed!"

Even people noted for their piety and prayer life, like Augustine's mother, Monica, find that their prayers of the moment do not always receive an immediate answer.

Is No a Valid Answer?

In his play *Antony and Cleopatra* William Shakespeare said: "We, ignorant of ourselves, beg often our own harms, which the wise powers deny us for our good: so find we profit by the losing of our prayers."

Once when questioned by newspaper reporters about his golf game, evangelist Billy Graham said, "God answers my prayers everywhere except on the golf course!" In his book *Billy Graham Answers Your Questions* he said, " 'No' is certainly an answer of love on the part of our Heavenly Father when we ask Him for things which are not really for our good or for His glory."

As the father of six children, I have seen scads of Christmas lists petitioning me to give a variety of things. When the children were little, the lists would include general desires: teddy bear, wagon, train set, doll. But as they grow and become more exposed to the spirit of the age, their lists become more sophisticated. Last year, Patricia, my ten-year-old, presented me with a list of eighty-six items; she had cut out toy-catalog pictures of each thing and included a note as to color, size, brand, price and which stores sold each item.

She prays exactly like I do!

And here, being an earthly father myself helps me understand a little about how my heavenly Father handles the lists I fax to him by prayer. Yes, I can afford to give a Daisy Air Rifle—but I'm not about to!

You see, while the character of God does include such big-sounding attributes as omnipresence, omniscience and omnipotence, he also has one we tend to forget about.

God has common sense.

Of course he denies some of your requests. You would too if you understood the implications of what you are asking for!

— thirteen —

My Prayer Versus God's Will

If I pray for what I want,

but God only sends what **he** *wants,*

then why bother to pray?

I RAN OUT OF MONEY BEFORE I RAN OUT OF MONTH.

Like my father used to tell the cashier when he'd hand her the money to pay a bill, "Don't worry about it; there's plenty more where that went."

I sat at my desk puzzling over a checkbook that refused to balance. I worried and prayed and worried some more. Nothing in the world felt more important to me than the financial problems I was facing. They overshadowed everything.

Then Patricia, my youngest daughter, burst in with a shout of joy. Her name had just been announced on television. Her entry in the WNFT Channel 47 Kids' Club coloring contest had been selected. She had won a five-minute shopping spree at a local toy store!

Leaving bills, checkbook and yellow scribble pad on the desk, we called the television station to confirm the news. It was true! Patricia ended up with eight shopping baskets full of goodies, and a brand-new scooter too. She had more toys than she'd ever owned before, and piles to share with all her friends, and boxes full to take to the poor kids at the rescue mission where she worked as a volunteer once a week.

What happened to that pile of bills I was so worried about?

I can't remember!

We made out somehow. But the only thing I vividly remember about that day is my daughter's joy.

Prayer and the Will of God

That incident reminds me of how prayer works with the will of God. I will have an overwhelming problem—one that fills the horizon and blocks my view of everything else. One that I pray and worry over ad nauseam.

Nothing is more important to me than that problem.

Then here comes the will of God!

Usually it has nothing to do with the thing I thought was so important just a few minutes before. It does not solve the problem that concerned me. But God brings about some happy circumstance that pushes my "major concern" into the background.

He has not answered my specific prayers about the problem.

He has eclipsed them.

What used to be important isn't anymore. It's still there; but it has faded to insignificant in the light of God's will.

Usually, but not always immediately, God's will involves a very happy thing. He is on our side. For some reason he likes us. He wants good stuff for us.

What God wills to give us is exactly what we would have chosen ourselves if only we'd known the whole story.

François Fénelon, whom I've quoted before, said,

When you cease to be eager for anything save the glory of God, and the fulfillment of his good pleasure, your peace will be as deep as the ocean. . . . The indecision of your mind, which cannot be steadfast [even] when things are settled, causes you a great deal of utterly useless trouble, and hinders you in God's ways. You do not go on, you simply go round and round in a circle of unprofitable fancies.

The moment that you think of nothing save God's will you will cease to fear, and there will be no hindrance in your way.

Unfortunately, the person we usually hear talking about God's will is someone trying to recruit us to traipse off to a mission in Bangladesh or a college in Cleveland.

Also, it often seems that the people who urge me to pray for God's will have been trying to discourage me from doing something or the other that I wanted to do. "You've got to be careful, John," they say. "It's so easy to miss God's will."

That's pure hogwash. You'd have to be a bullheaded ninny and work hard at it to thwart the will of the Creator of the universe!

Isaiah said,

A highway shall be there, and a road,

And it shall be called

the Highway of Holiness.

The unclean shall not pass over it,

But it shall be for others.

Whoever walks the road,

although a fool,

Shall not go astray. (Isaiah 35:8 NKJV)

No need to be timid. God has given you a life to live with joy. Take a bath. Roll in the leaves. Run. Study. Marry. Pray. Witness. Enjoy. All sorts of good stuff is God's will for you.

Sure you will make mistakes. Who doesn't? The only critter that can't ever fall down is a worm. But a Christian's goofs are not fatal, soul-destroying ones.

If the LORD delights in a man's way,

    he makes his steps firm;
  though he stumble, he will not fall,
    for the LORD upholds him with his hand. . . .
For the LORD loves the just
  and will not forsake his faithful ones. (Psalm 37:23-24, 28)

Relax. Even if you're such a klutz that you need a keeper, you will not miss God's will.

You've got a Keeper.

If you get off the track, don't worry. He will set you straight; he's good at that. "Whether you turn to the right or to the left, your ears will hear a voice behind you, saying, 'This is the way; walk in it' " (Isaiah 30:21).

God's Will and Pain

When we pray, "Thy will be done on earth as it is in heaven," we are praying for good stuff. When we pray for God's will to be done in our lives or in a specific situation, we are praying for a happy result. We are not pitting the good we want against some harsh dictate from heaven and then surrendering to overwhelming force.

Where did we ever get a sad idea like that?

As a member of a large extended family, I have spent a great deal of time in hospital corridors with clusters of friends, uncles, aunts and cousins awaiting news about some other relative who has fallen ill or been in a sawmill accident, train wreck or car crash. Inevitably, when the news is bad, when the person is pronounced incurable or dies, someone in the group always says piously, "It must be God's will."

I hardly ever heard that phrase used in any other situation; so I grew up thinking that God only willed bad stuff in hospital corridors.

Every so often the picture that comes unbidden to my mind when I think about God's will is a visit to the dentist. Sure, the man wishes me no ill—in fact, he's doing some long-term good for me—but just the same, I'm afraid that he's going to hurt me.

What a sad and limited view of God.

We don't need to be scared of God. God's will does sometimes involve pain, but usually it involves joy—both immediate and long-range.

Remember the lines of Scripture you hear in every Christmas pageant: "Fear not: for, behold, I bring you good tidings of great joy. . . . Glory to God in the highest, and on earth peace, good will toward men!" the angels announce (Luke 2:10, 14 KJV).

The assumption that God's will always involves something bad comes in part, I think, from the high drama of Christ's prayer in Gethsemane and in part from a passage found in John's first letter (5:13-14, which we'll look at later).

Knowing that he faced crucifixion, Jesus prayed, "My Father, if it is possible, may this cup be taken from me. Yet not as I will, but as you will." And a second time he prayed, "My Father, if it is not possible for this cup to be taken away unless I drink it, may your will be done" (Matthew 26:39, 42).

Saving us hurt him.

He knew it would. Jesus knew exactly what he was getting into. No doubt God's will in offering us the gift of salvation cost him excruciating pain.

He did it anyhow.

And a servant is no better than his master; God's will does sometimes bring us intense and immediate pain.

How can we deal with that?

"Let us fix our eyes on Jesus, the author and perfecter of our faith, who for the joy set before him endured the cross. . . . Consider him who endured . . . so that you will not grow weary and lose heart" (Hebrews 12:2-3).

God's will does indeed sometimes involve present suffering. There are times when he takes your mind off petty troubles by sending a bigger trouble.

Sometimes God's will does hurt—but it's worth it.

St. Peter advises, "Those who suffer according to God's will should commit themselves to their faithful Creator and continue to do good" (1 Peter 4:19).

The Happy Will of God

But while pain and suffering may be involved, the general message of Scripture is that God's will involves happy stuff. Verse after verse links happy words, pleasure and joyous events with the will of God.

Look at just three instances from Paul's writings:

Do not conform any longer to the pattern of this world, but be transformed by the renewing of your mind. Then you will be able to test and approve what God's will is—his good, pleasing and perfect will. (Romans 12:2)

Pray that I may be rescued from the unbelievers in Judea . . . so that by God's will I may come to you with joy and together with you be refreshed. (Romans 15:31-32)

Be joyful always; pray continually; give thanks in all circumstances, for this is God's will for you in Christ Jesus. (1 Thessalonians 5:16-18)

Praying for God's will to be done does not mean that we give up in exasperation. God is not a dentist. His good will is not something to fear. "For you did not receive a spirit that makes you a slave again to fear, but you received the Spirit of sonship. And by him we cry, '*Abba,* Father.' . . . The Spirit intercedes for the saints in accordance with God's will" (Romans 8:15, 27).

Does God Will Train Wrecks?

Even knowing that God's will is best and that he wills good, pleasant, happy outcomes to the issues I pray about, I still sometimes feel cheated and tricked.

On the one hand I read all those promises that if I ask anything,

God will give it; then on the other hand I read a passage like this: This is the confidence we have in approaching God: that if we ask anything *according to his will,* he hears us. And if we know that he hears us—whatever we ask—we know that we have what we asked of him. (1 John 5:14-15) Has God given himself a loophole to wiggle out of the gospel's promises?

Is the deal this: that I can ask whatever I want, but he really does not intend to give it unless it's something that *he* wants?

If he's going to do whatever he pleases anyhow, why did he invite me to ask in the first place? If I'm not going to get what I request unless I ask what he wants me to ask, then I might as forget the whole thing.

That's the way my friend Phil felt.

Phil had gone to meet his girlfriend's train. Something went wrong, and the train did not stop when it reached the end of the tracks. The engine and several cars smashed into the terminal building. Many people were killed. Phil's girlfriend was severely injured. Standing with a bunch of flowers still clutched in his hands, he saw her mangled form carried out. In the hospital, he stayed by her bedside for days, begging God to spare her life.

She died.

"I'll never pray again," Phil told me. "Why should I? He took her even though I prayed. He pays no attention. Praying is a waste of breath."

Poor Phil.

What horrible pain.

Most of the times I've heard someone question, "Why doesn't God answer my prayers?" the question has been born out of pain.

I have no answer to that pain. In fact, my own pain causes me to ask the same question.

One of the greatest Baptist preachers of a former age, Charles Haddon Spurgeon, wrestled with this same pain as he prayed about the impending death of someone he cared about. Spurgeon said:

> Many times Jesus and His people pull against one another in prayer. You bend your knee in prayer and say, "Father, I will that Thy saints be with me where I am"; Christ says, "Father, I will that they also whom Thou hast given Me, be with Me where I am."
>
> Thus the disciple is at cross-purposes with his Lord.
>
> The soul cannot be in both places; the beloved one cannot be with Christ and with you too. Now, which pleader shall win the day? If you had your choice; if the King should step from His throne, and say, "Here are two supplicants praying in opposition to one another, which shall be answered?" Oh! I am sure, though it were agony, you would start from your feet, and say, "Jesus, not my will, but Thine be done." You would give up your prayer for your loved one's life, if you could realize the thought that Christ is praying in the opposite direction—"Father, I will that they also, whom Thou hast given Me, be with Me where I am."
>
> Lord, Thou shalt have them. By faith we let them go.

God's Will Rubs Off on Us

Long ago, I dated a beautiful young woman from Australia. Nothing came of it. She had better taste. But I recall an odd phenomenon: any time I talked with her, for even a few minutes, I'd pick up her distinctive accent and begin to talk like her.

Closer to home, whenever I'd go back to the farm and visit my grandparents, before long I'd start saying things like "I reckon I'll help Aunt Annie tote in her suitcase, then sit a spell in the rocker."

I think it's true of anyone: whenever we have close contact with a strong personality, we begin to pick up that person's speech and character patterns.

Praying brings a Christian into conscious contact with God. Being Christian means being realigned with God. Opening the door to Christ does let him inside us—and contact with him changes us.

Stroke a knife blade with a magnet, and the blade becomes magnetic. Stroke a screwdriver, and it also becomes magnetic. A paper clip does the same thing. Each tool retains its individuality—the knife still cuts, the clip still holds paper—but something is added.

Prayer rubs us against God.

Our internal alignment changes. The magnetic attraction of Christ draws us to some things and pushes us away from others. We retain our individuality; we are still totally ourselves—but with a new polarity.

Contact with God makes you—yes, you—godly.

His will and your will begin to dovetail, to blend. The good you want and the good God wills start to mesh.

You are praying, asking anything you desire, with newer, deeper, stronger desires. And you are asking according to the will of God, because that will is not at cross-purposes and at odds with your will.

Love lines you up.

French mystic Marie Guyon observed that when two harps stand in the same room, if you pluck a string on one, that same musical note begins to sound from the other one.

That's praying in the will of God.

Good vibes!

— fourteen —

Hurry Up
and Waite

If I have an urgent need

and pray but nothing happens

. . . what then?

G OD IS ETERNAL.
 The Scripture tells us that over and over. I am the Lord; I change not. Jesus Christ is the same yesterday, today and forever. The Bible says he is the first and the last, the Alpha and Omega. The Ancient of Days. The Everlasting Father. The great I AM.

God never changes.

If God were to change, either he would get better than he already is or (I don't know how else to say this) he would get *worse* than he already is.

God does not change for the better; he is already perfect. Neither does he change for the worse; he is holy.

We and the world around us are neither perfect nor holy. We change. Our circumstances change. The people around us change.

And change is measured by time.

To change the position of your finger from here to there, no matter how quickly you do it, takes a certain amount of time. The blink of an eye—the eyelid flicking from open to shut to open again—takes a certain amount of time. The speed of light, the fastest thing we know, is a measurement of distance in terms of time.

We view time as change, a sequence of events. We see time either as a fast change of things, like a week's vacation, or as a slow change, like payday finally getting here.

Because we view time as movement in a sequence, one event following another, we see any event as being caused by events preceding it; and we see that this event will in turn cause others still to come. The thing that is happening to me now was caused by something that happened before, and this thing that's going on now is sure to have consequences.

We pray in order to affect the future consequences of past or present actions and events.

☐ Dear Lord, Joe is still sick; please heal him.

☐ Michelle is lost; please save her.

☐ Our marriage is breaking up; please don't let George leave me!

☐ The rent is coming due and I don't have money to pay it; please help me find a job soon.

☐ The letter from the lawyer came today; I need to know what to do quick!

Urgent Prayers to a Slow God

I often find the crisis situations I pray about paralyzing. When I see no immediate answer to my prayer, anxiety consumes me. I feel that all my resources are exhausted. You know the feeling. If we had some bacon, we could cook bacon and eggs for breakfast, if we had some eggs. I feel tied hand and foot, helpless.

When I feel this way, it's some comfort to realize that Jesus knows what it feels like; he also was nailed down hand and foot.

Because we regard time the way we do, naturally we see some things as urgent. And we pray urgent prayers. We sometimes panic in the sense of urgency we feel. We are certain that the event that needs changing must be changed *right now,* because if it isn't a disaster already, it will be by Thursday!

Hurry, God. Hurry! Rush! Rush! Things are getting out of control! Really out of hand!

But God sees time differently from the way we do.

Nothing panics God. Nothing dismays him. Nothing is out of his control. Nothing gets out of his hand. Nothing rushes him.

He sees the beginning and end of all things. For him, time is not a sequence of surprising events, sudden changes and urgent situations; he sees all time as a single unit. He is stable and in him we live our lives and move through time and exist in eternity.

Nothing is urgent to God. And God's cool, controlled lack of urgency makes it appear that he is callous when we feel panicked by the crisis of the moment. When we pray and God's sense of timing overrules *our* sense of timing, it appears to us that he may never answer our prayer.

There's an old joke that goes like this:

MAN: Lord, I know that you made the earth and stars and that a thousand years in your sight are but a minute, and that you have all power and all riches, and all the cattle on a thousand hills are yours; will you please give me a million dollars?

LORD: Certainly, I'll be glad to. Just wait a minute.

God's patience, his sense of the proper time to do things, often looks to me as though it's neglect. God does not jump when I snap, so I get impatient and frustrated. He has hurt my feelings.

But Prayer Is Supposed to Work!

Still, Scripture promises that prayer works. So I'm tempted to begin a campaign of prayer designed to force God into action, to pray longer and harder and louder about the situation that so obviously needs urgent attention. I give him numerous instant replays of my prayer in case he missed it the first eighteen times.

Jesus said: "When you pray, do not keep on babbling like pagans, for they think they will be heard because of their many words. Do not be like them, for your Father knows what you need before you ask him" (Matthew 6:7-8).

Jesus labels vain repetition as "heathen" or "pagan"; he says that such babbling is useless. The Living God is not ignorant; he knows what we need, and he's ready to respond before we know ourselves.

Let's give God credit for some intelligence. When we pray, we are talking to Someone who knows and cares about us. Do we really think the broken-record tactic of assertiveness training is likely to bully him into giving in to our demands?

Now, *persistence* in prayer is an altogether different thing. Persistence in prayer means that we continue to hope, that we do not give up in discouragement. In the parable of the poor widow and the unjust judge, Jesus commends persistence: "Will not God bring about justice for his chosen ones, who cry out to him day and night? Will he keep putting them off? I tell you, he will see that they get justice, and quickly" (Luke 18:7-8).

Remember, Christians pray at the invitation of God. He initiates prayer. He encourages us to pray for certain things, and he actually commands us to pray for others.

Barbara White, religion editor of the *Florida Times-Union,* says, "Perseverance in prayer is simply continued obedience even through repeated failures." That makes sense to me. Even when I have no idea why my prayers are not answered as quickly as I expect them to be, I still have the obligation to continue praying. God knows my needs. He understands what's going on.

As Mother Teresa has often said, "God has not called us to succeed, he has called us to be faithful." And being faithful takes time.

We need to persevere. "You have need of endurance, so that after you have done the will of God, you may receive the promise" (Hebrews 10:36 NKJV).

Delayed Answers
When God's people were enslaved in Egypt, they prayed to be delivered.

After four hundred years of their crying and groaning under cruel taskmasters, God eventually got around to it. He exercised his power and came on strong with plagues of flies and fleas, a pillar of cloud by day and a pillar of fire by night. He parted the sea and zapped the Egyptians.

He demonstrated power to answer prayer in an undeniable way.

All well and good for the folks who saw it, but what about those first guys, the ones who had prayed four hundred years earlier? Their prayers were answered in God's own sweet time, but were they around to appreciate it?

No. They were sand-dried mummies by the time their prayers for deliverance were answered.

Here's another case of a long-delayed answer to a prayer.

In the annals of prayer, few people stand out more than George Müller, who established an orphanage in Bristol, England, during the 1850s and over many years fed thousands of children without any income other than what he prayed for daily.

His diary contains dozens of instances of prayer answered immediately for each day's immediate needs. For instance, one morning when there was no milk for the children's breakfast, Müller went to prayer, and as he prayed a milk wagon broke an axle right at the corner. The driver, unable to finish his deliveries and afraid the milk might spoil, donated his load to the orphanage.

Once when twenty-eight new orphans arrived and there were no plates to feed them on, Müller prayed and a woman who was moving to a new home arrived at the door with a donation of used kitchen supplies, including twenty-eight spoons, twenty-eight forks, twenty-eight table knives, twenty-eight cups, twenty-eight plates and twenty-eight bowls.

However, not every answer came to Müller immediately. Toward the end of his life he wrote, "I have been praying for sixty-three years and eight months for one man's conversion. He has not converted yet, but he will be! How can it be otherwise? There is the unchanging promise of Jehovah, and on that I rest."

Müller died. But before he could be buried, the man he'd prayed for all those years made a profession of Christian faith!

Müller had once said of prayer, "The great point is never to give up until the answer comes."

Terry Waite Waits

Some people think that the long delay that can come between the first time we pray and the time we see an answer is God's time for teaching us something.

As Anglican envoy Terry Waite negotiated to free hostages captured by Muslim terrorists, the terrorists kidnapped Waite himself on January 20, 1987. They chained him to the wall in a sealed room for almost four years of solitary confinement.

Waite questioned why God had allowed this trouble; he was a Christian trying to do good. In an interview with Knight-Ridder Newspapers writer Peggy Landers after his release, Waite said that while he never lost his faith during captivity, he did ask perplexing questions. He said that when serious trouble comes, doubt lingers in the shadows of the staunchest belief.

The Shiite fundamentalists did allow him a few books: Hemingway, Virgil, the Koran and a Bible. For a time, Waite found Hemingway more comforting than the Bible! In fact, some Bible stories of captives being set free discouraged him—"why them and not me?" he wondered.

In reading the New Testament, Waite said, "One could get a bit irritated; you read about people in prison and how the bars of their prison are broken open and they are put free, and you think, 'Goodness me, here am I year after year.' "

Waite had plenty of time to think and pray in his cell. When he read the story in John's Gospel about Jesus changing water into wine, he gained a new perspective on his situation.

"The real inner meaning of that story came clear to me, which is that a conversion of your circumstances has to take place deep within your self.

"Like water into wine, the most miserable situation and most miserable surroundings can be transformed—if you allow the transformation process to take place inside you. Although that's not easy, it is possible. Slowly. Slowly," he said.

In the next room, a generator throbbed away, venting fumes into Waite's cell. He developed lung problems which would not allow him to lie down and breathe at the same time. He could not sleep for days on end.

His prayers changed; because of his own misery, he began to pray more for other people in tormenting circumstances.

I'd say, "Well, there are all those other people suffering around the world and here's a chance, somehow, to link my suffering with theirs—mentally and spiritually." And one would pray and almost go off in a trance-like state, and not feel alone. . . . That says something about the reality of the spiritual life, and the reality of being linked through prayer with other people.

Prayer is not, to me, so much asking something for yourself, but somehow trying to be linked with God and hopefully with other people in a way that has some meaning and substance to it. And I think that is something I learned from this experience.

After 1,763 days in captivity, Waite was released in November 1991.

"A lot of people look to Christian faith almost, one might say, to ease suffering. Well, in some ways it *doesn't* ease suffering. Suffering has to be faced and experienced. What it does do is give you the strength to go through it, to endure it, to proceed. And that seems to me to be the whole message of the cross, of the crucifixion," he said.

It appears to me that when God delays a specific answer to one of our specific prayers for a long time, he sends us a sort of secondary answer—from his power he sends us the strength to endure.

To deliver us from our particular cruel taskmaster, to convert the person we despair of ever seeing converted, to set us free requires no more effort from God than dropping a brick. He is the Help of the Helpless.

We have need of patience so that after we have done the will of God we may still receive the promise.

When "Wait" Is the Answer
Sometimes "Wait" may be the answer to our prayers.

But Lord, I hate to wait. I hate it, I hate it, I hate it! I want my cut of the pie. I want a large slice and I want it now!

Now. Now. Now . . .

There, now that I've said what I really feel about the subject, let's consider the problem of waiting and prayer practically, rationally and theologically.

There are a lot of different kinds of waiting.

Ruth may lose one of her breasts. She's waiting for some test results before she'll know. She waits in apprehension.

The judge found William guilty, then announced, "Appear in this court Friday morning, two weeks from today's date, for sentencing." William faced anything from probation to a year in jail, but he told me, "I wish she'd gone ahead and passed sentence. This waiting is the worst part."

The following day, another of my friends joyfully proclaimed, "I've won an award! The review committee just called to make sure I'll be at the banquet Saturday night. I don't know if I've won first, second or third, and I won't know till the banquet—I can hardly wait!"

When she was five, my daughter Eve often rocked in her little chair with the Sears catalog open in her lap to the toy pages, starry-eyed over a Christmas that was still months away. She waited in anticipation.

You make an important phone call, and a secretary puts you on hold; you hold and hold and hold. The train chugs across the crossing until you finally see the caboose; then it clatters to a halt and begins to creep backward. You need your car, but the dealer has to order the part, and apparently there's a dock strike in Yokohama.

Waiting is part of life—an aggravating part. Whether we wait in apprehension, apathy or anticipation, waiting bothers us. We are an impatient race.

Naturally, when we pray, we want an immediate answer. We see the urgency of our request and have a hard time understanding when God's answer seems to be "Wait." We all hate to wait.

Waiting means the delay of our personal plans. It means our forced submission to another's will or to the dictates of circumstance. Above all, waiting means that something is out of our control.

When we pray and then have to wait, we can feel frustrated and may be tempted to "speed things up." But if we are looking forward to some future good, anticipation actually sharpens the pleasure. In fact, the pleasure of the event can be diminished by *not* waiting—as in the case of the engaged couple who jump the gun before their marriage or the prowling child who discovers all the toys in the closet and is therefore left without a single surprise on Christmas morning.

Waiting on God
The Bible tells us no fewer than fifty-four times to wait for God. In

fact, everybody in the Bible seems to associate some waiting with prayer. King Solomon said, "Wait for the LORD, and he will deliver you" (Proverbs 20:22). The prophet Micah said, "I wait for God my Savior; my God will hear me" (Micah 7:7). King David said, "Truly my soul silently waits for God; from Him comes my salvation" (Psalm 62:1 NKJV). Paul said, "We ourselves, who have the first-fruits of the Spirit, groan inwardly as we wait eagerly for our adoption as sons, the redemption of our bodies" (Romans 8:23).

Since God is not the author of confusion, it's obvious that these holy instructions should not involve the annoyance, frustration and mental turmoil we commonly associate with waiting.

When we pray and nothing seems to happen, and we have to wait and wait for an answer, it may help if we understand what the Bible means by waiting.

One of the most commonly used Hebrew words translated "wait" means to bind together by twisting. This word is used in Psalm 25:3, "Let no one who waits on You be ashamed" (NKJV). Picture the intertwined strands of a rope. Our interests are to be so interwoven with God's that one strand does not move without the other.

The psalmist David sometimes uses a Hebrew word that indicates waiting in the midst of pain and anguish. "Be still before the LORD and wait patiently for him" (Psalm 37:7). This same Hebrew word is used to refer to a woman writhing with birth pangs; she endures intense pain but anticipates the joyful delivery of her baby.

Paul uses a Greek word for "wait" which conveys the idea of dwelling, abiding or staying in a given place or relationship. "You turned to God from idols to serve the living and true God, and to wait for his Son from heaven, whom he raised from the dead" (1 Thessalonians 1:9-10).

Paul sometimes uses a different word for "wait" which means to sit near, to attend as a servant, to stay alert to see when and where service is needed. Other Hebrew and Greek words translated "wait" convey the following meanings: to scrutinize with expectant hope (like a cat at a mouse hole); to expect fully, to accept from some source (like a drowning swimmer who catches glimpses of the approaching lifeguard); to be stopped short with astonishment (as when your name is announced as a sweepstakes winner).

Annoyance Has No Place

Scriptural waiting has no room for annoyance and irritation. To the contrary, the Bible connects joy with waiting for God's answers to our prayers.

Behold, this is our God;
We have waited for Him,
    and He will save us.
This is the LORD;
We have waited for Him;
We will be glad and rejoice
    in His salvation. (Isaiah 25:9 NKJV)

Waiting on the Lord anticipates unimaginable happiness, not aggravation. "For since the beginning of the world men have not heard, nor perceived by the ear, neither hath the eye seen, O God, beside thee, what he hath prepared for him that waiteth for him" (Isaiah 64:4 KJV).

When Scripture tells us to wait on the Lord, it is instructing us to be a certain kind of person—a person who endures troubles with the hope of Christ; a person who is determined to hang on for God; a person who abides in his given place, staying alert to serve; a person who intertwines her own will with God's will in the warp and woof of everyday life, not just in panic situations; in short, a crucified person, like our Lord. Thus we are to pray—and wait for God's answer to come in God's time.

— fifteen —

Hearing a Little Voice

If God did speak to me

during prayer,

would I hear him?

S OMETIMES I THINK THAT GOD IS NOT ANSWERING MY PRAYERS—
but the real trouble is that I'm not listening to his answer.

Prayer is a two-person conversation, and when we pray, we need to learn to listen for God's voice. If we don't, how will we know whether he is answering us or not?

Several people in the Bible had their prayers answered by dreams or visions in the night. Is that how God speaks to us?

Dreams and Urges

I don't remember the day I first met my wife; she doesn't remember our first meeting either. We don't remember meeting each other because we were both members of a large young people's group at church and became aware of each other's existence gradually.

However, I vividly remember how I became convinced that I ought to get acquainted with this woman and pursue her. That conviction came to me in a dream. I believe that God spoke to me in that dream.

Now I must hasten to add a major disclaimer: *I believe that God hardly ever speaks to me or anyone else in dreams.* In my experience, the dream about Ginny was an exception, a never-repeated exception.

Normally I'd be crazy to act on the basis of a dream or to think my prayers are answered by a dream. For instance, last night before bed I was praying about a financial problem; I fell asleep praying and dreamed that I was naked in the woods, where I chased down a deer on foot, killed it with my bare hands, ripped it open and ate the raw, bloody meat.

Was God answering my prayer about finances by sending me this dream about becoming a fat Tarzan? Hardly! It would take a mighty strong vine to hold *my* weight!

If God seldom answers our prayers by dreams, then what about urges—strong feelings that I want to do something, that I ought to do a certain thing, that I *need* to do it? Does God send us strong mental impressions in answer to our prayers?

I think that he sometimes, but rarely, does.

Ginny and I often pray to be sensitive to God's voice, to be aware of his guidance when he wants us to do—or not do—something. Once about 3:00 a.m., I woke up suddenly with the sure knowledge that my uncle and aunt were in grave danger. I don't know how I knew this, I just did.

I woke Ginny and told her. We felt that God had warned me about my aunt and uncle's danger. We prayed for their protection and decided that I'd better drive over to their house right away and rescue them. I threw on my clothes and drove rapidly across town to their home where I found . . . everybody safe and well and sound asleep.

Odd, isn't it?

What kind of mind game was God playing with me to mislead me like that?

Or perhaps God was not speaking to me at all. Maybe this urge had nothing to do with God's guidance. Maybe it was the result of the pizza and chocolate ice cream I'd eaten the previous evening. Yet there have been other times when I felt the same sort of urge but it did seem, as things worked out, that God was speaking to me.

Once I was driving a tractor-trailer truck cross-country, and, as was my habit, I prayed as I drove. In prayer I felt that God would have me turn off the main route across Ohio and drive north. No reason given. I debated it a while, then started north away from the interstate. Drove a few miles. Nothing happened.

I decided this was dumb and pulled into a truck stop for supper before heading back where I belonged.

While I was eating, another truck driver walked up to my table. "Look, buddy," he said, "I've got to talk to somebody. Could I sit here and talk to you?"

He had been driving along a different road, crying over his family problems as he drove, when he felt an urge to leave his route and come to the intersection where we met. Neither of us had even known there was a truck stop on that road.

He left that place as a Christian with hope. He planned to go back to his wife. He said our conversation had helped.

I suspect the urges to turn off the road that he and I both felt were indeed urges from God. An odd thought occurs to me: by obeying my urge, I became an answer to that guy's prayers! If I had not followed the urge, his prayer would have remained unanswered, at least by me.

In these two incidents from years ago, the urges I experienced felt exactly the same. In the first case, maybe the urge I thought had come from God really came from eating all that pizza; in the second case, truck stops are where trucks stop—nothing miraculous about drivers meeting there.

How do you tell the difference between God's voice in answering your prayers and the voice of undigested pizza? Does he really speak to us nowadays? I hear my own voice in prayer loudly, but how do I hear God's still small voice?

Get your $19.95 ready, because here come a half-dozen preachy guidelines I find helpful as I try to hear God's voice.

1. God Has the Right to Speak

First, I acknowledge that God has priority. The Creator certainly has the right to direct and expect obedience from his created beings. He not only made us but also redeemed us with his own blood. What other boss can say that? God has double right to direct us.

2. For Heaven's Sake, Get a Life!

I believe that God has given me life, much as an art teacher might give a canvas to a student, and told me to paint my own picture on it. I am responsible for what goes in the picture, though he's always available for consultation and correction.

Like any earthly father, our heavenly Father sometimes tells his children to go outside and play. It's fine with him if you choose to play football, basketball or duck-duck-goose. He just wants us to have wholesome fun. I suspect that most of the career decisions we agonize over in prayer fall into this category.

3. Know the Rules

God has posted a few absolute laws on the studio wall concerning how I am to work. For instance, I'm forbidden to dip my brush in the next guy's paint jar. If I get an urge to do anything I know is morally wrong—contrary to the clearly posted rules—then I know for sure that is not the Lord's voice.

4. Read the Instructions

I believe that the Bible is God's Word and that the principles I discover when I read it regularly guide me in what to do in specific situations in my marriage, my business, my recreation and my life in general.

Now the Bible is a book; it is not a rabbit's foot or good-luck piece. Opening it at random and pointing to a verse to live today by makes as little sense as picking six random numbers to bet your money on—and produces just as few winners.

5. Who Said That?

I listen carefully to the counsel of other people. God can indeed speak through my wife, boss, mother-in-law, children or pastor.

Even a person who interrupts my prayers may very well be an answer to one of them. Archbishop Fénelon said, "The intruder whom God sends us serves to thwart our will, upset our plans, to make us crave more earnestly for silence and recollection, to teach us to sit loose to our own arrangements, our rest, our ease, our taste; to bend our will to that of others, to humble ourselves when impatience overcomes us under these annoyances, and to kindle in our hearts a greater thirst for God."

6. What Do You Feel Inside?

Then there's the matter of "burdens" in prayer. I take that term to mean the feeling that I ought to pray for someone or something even though the person or problem is no direct concern of mine. A burden for prayer often is a call to involvement. For instance, years ago I was riding a bus and noticed a group of people waiting at a bus stop in a downtown park at rush hour. They looked so tired and lost and lonely. Their faces haunted me for weeks. I began to pray for these strangers.

I suspect the burden to pray for them was the voice of God to me, because soon I began to strongly feel that somebody ought to do something to tell such people about God's love. Soon that transmuted into the impression that *I* ought to do something.

That was not what I wanted to hear.

Praying for the people at the bus stop was one thing, but it seemed God wanted me to get out there and—witness?

Me? I'm no preacher. I'm an Episcopalian, for heaven's sake. We don't do stuff like that! Why, at one local Episcopal church, when asked about an evangelism program, a vestryman said, "But we don't need to recruit members; we already have plenty."

Anyhow, after a long struggle—and not at all sure that I was really hearing God's voice in answer to my prayers—I did go to the park in my spare time. The shyest Christian in Jacksonville actually did speak to strangers and teach Bible lessons to groups at the bus stop.

This may well have been an exercise in masochism, or it may have been an answer to the prayer God originally laid as a burden on my heart. At any rate, over a period of about four years while I witnessed on the street, over a hundred people made a first-time profession of faith in Christ.

So I suspect that any time you see a need that bothers you enough to pray about it, God will tell you to do something about it personally.

No Voice Needed!

Once when my daughters Eve and Patricia were at a garage sale, they pooled their resources to scrape up five cents and bought a little prayer plaque for me. Now one of my greatest treasures, the plaque contains the words to a prayer I pray over and over:

Lord, help me to do
  What I can
    Where I am
      With what I have.

God certainly speaks to us by giving us clear-cut duties; there need be no special voice from heaven to tell you to take care of your aging parents, pay your bills, feed the hungry, do your job faithfully, tend your children, treat your employees generously, pray for government officials, feed and water the dog—such things are givens. If we listen as we pray, God will speak and answer us.

He speaks through Scripture, through other people, through circumstances, through opening doors, through closing doors, through dreams in the night, through light in the day.

— sixteen —

Unanswered Prayer and the Prince of This World

If the devil wanted to keep my prayer

from being answered, could he?

GOD WILLS CERTAIN THINGS. YOU AND I WILL CERTAIN THINGS. IN prayer our wills can blend with his will. But unfortunately, another will can spoil this blending. Satan also has a will and a way in this fallen world of ours.

Anybody Else?
Youth minister D. C. Veale tells this story about prayer.

Once upon a time, a man walking in the forest came to a high cliff and looked over the edge. He saw a three-hundred-foot drop beneath him, with only one small branch jutting out about halfway down the sheer rock wall.

Suddenly his foot slipped and he fell 150 feet down—but managed to grab that one small branch.

Looking down, he saw that the cliff ended in a rocky ravine at the bottom; looking up, he could only see a few trees clustered at the top.

"Help! Help!" he screamed. "Is anybody up there?"

A shining cloud formed in the sky, and a voice answered from the cloud, "It's okay. Don't be afraid. I am here."

"Who is that talking?" called the man.

"This is God. I am with you," said the voice from the cloud.

"Wonderful!" said the hiker. "I'm saved! What do you want me to do?"

"Let go of the branch," said the voice.

The man looked down into the deep ravine. He looked up at the clifftop.

He looked down into the ravine again.

"Help! Help!" he shouted. "Is there anybody else up there?"

I think that story reveals Satan's basic attack on the prayers of humankind. He encourages us to call for "anybody else" instead of God.

And we do.

All too often we do.

Okay. Sure. I can see that. But if God knows my needs, and if he cares about me, and if he is all-powerful, then why does he let the devil ever hinder even one of my prayers? I want to think about that problem a bit.

My Root Prayer

I have a couple of different root prayers.

A root prayer is what I call a sort of mellow, laid-back, every-thing-I-want-out-of-life-for-my-general-comfort-and-convenience prayer, a prayer to cover all the bases when nothing major is going wrong at the moment.

One of my root prayers goes a bit like this:

Dear Lord, I'd like for everyone to enjoy a good life. For married couples to love each other and get along. For people to have plenty

*to eat and a nice clean, cozy, warm place to live, a home with no
stopped-up plumbing. For workers to enjoy what they are doing
and to earn decent salaries on their jobs; for work to be challeng-
ing and not a drudge. For students to be excited by their studies
and eager to learn new things. For everybody to have a car that
runs good, not necessarily a new car but one that doesn't overheat
and make like Moby Dick. And a home where they are happy.
And I'd like for people to tolerate their differences and accept each
other. And for the air to be clean, the water pure and the forests
lush. For the roads to be safe and the businesspeople honest. I'd
like for young people to enjoy just as much adventure as they
want, and for old people to be as secure as they want, and for
little kids to play together without fighting and to have fun. I'd
like a world without war, disease, poverty or hassle. I'd like to
sit by my fire with my pipe and a good book and savory smells
drifting out from the kitchen and my kind of music on the radio
while the kids listen to their trash in the family room, and I hear
them laugh every once in a while . . . That's the kind of life I pray
for, and I want it not just for my family but for everybody. Amen.*

Your vision of a good, satisfying life may differ in details from mine,
but I don't think my prayer is too radical. Do you?

I think I'm making a perfectly reasonable request of God when
I pray this sort of root prayer.

Universal Root Prayers

Not only do I think my prayer is reasonable, but I think it is
scriptural. You know, land flowing with milk and honey, every man
dwelling under his own fig tree, love your neighbor, that sort of
thing.

St. Paul says that the whole created world earnestly prays this
sort of universal prayer:

For the created universe waits with eager expectation for God's
sons to be revealed. It was made the victim of frustration, not

by its own choice, but because of him who made it so; yet always there was hope, because the universe itself is to be freed from the shackles of mortality and enter upon the liberty and splendour of the children of God. Up to the present, we know, the whole created universe groans in all its parts as if in the pangs of childbirth. (Romans 8:19-22 NEB)

Yes, indeed.

Down deep, everybody prays for a good, prosperous life with just enough peace, just enough excitement, just enough security, just enough adventure; with plenty of novelty and plenty of satisfaction.

A wise man, I think it was G. K. Chesterton, said, "The chief end of all human endeavor is to be happy at home."

A good, satisfying life is what we all want.

This is what we all pray for. This is what the Scripture says God intends for the world to be like. This is the norm—but most of us only catch brief glimpses of the good life, while many in this world never see it at all.

Why aren't our prayers for the good life answered? Why do the people who seem to achieve the good life die in pain and leave it behind them?

What we truly want, the good life, satisfying life, abundant life, what the Bible calls eternal life—that life God does promise to give us. "For God so loved the world that he gave his one and only Son, that whoever believes in him shall not perish but have eternal life. For God did not send his Son into the world to condemn the world, but to save the world" (John 3:16-17).

So we see that our root prayers will be answered—eventually.

But why not here?

Why not now?

Because—because we live in a battle zone.

That's right. We're in the Lord's army. This world is not our home; we are on temporary assignment in enemy-occupied territory.

Combat Conditions

What would be a perfectly reasonable, normal lifestyle in peace-time, soldiers give up for the duration of a war. Combat troops don't live in the comfortable homes where they would live normally; during the emergency they live in tents and eat field rations. They leave their firesides and families to face loneliness, hardship and danger. They stand a good chance of being killed or horribly mutilated.

And we, too, are fighting a monstrous enemy who has a multi-tude of troops.

St. Paul explains how this fact relates to prayer in less than a thousand words:

Put on the full armor of God so that you can take your stand against the devil's schemes. For our struggle is not against flesh and blood, but against the rulers, against the authorities, against the powers of this dark world and against the spiritual forces of evil in the heavenly realms. Therefore put on the full armor of God, so that when the day of evil comes, you may be able to stand your ground, and after you have done everything, to stand. Stand firm then, with the belt of truth buckled around your waist, with the breastplate of righteousness in place, and with your feet fitted with the readiness that comes from the gospel of peace. In addition to all this, take up the shield of faith, with which you can extinguish all the flaming arrows of the evil one. Take the helmet of salvation and the sword of the Spirit, which is the word of God. And pray in the Spirit on all occasions with all kinds of prayers and requests. With this in mind, be alert and always keep on praying for all the saints. (Ephesians 6:11-18)

Yes, the devil and his spiritual forces of evil have invaded and occupied God's world, and as we pray on all occasions with all kinds of prayers, these demons rage against our prayers.

The enemy of our souls usually fights through subterfuge, but he also sometimes launches all-out frontal assaults with flaming arrows, massive carnage, disaster, disease, Scuds, sword and fire. But in addition to demon forces, Satan uses human traitors. These human traitors are the reason the war has been prolonged.

St. Peter said, "Do not forget this one thing, dear friends: With the Lord a day is like a thousand years, and a thousand years are like a day. The Lord is not slow in keeping his promise, as some understand slowness. He is patient with you, not wanting anyone to perish, but everyone to come to repentance" (2 Peter 3:8-9).

You see, our General could have nuked the demon invaders ages ago. But he wants the human rebels taken alive—and turned.

Why should even a single inhabitant of God's world be lost to Satan?

God's attitude about this enrages Satan. Peter warned, "Be self-controlled and alert. Your enemy the devil prowls around like a roaring lion looking for someone to devour. Resist him, standing firm in the faith, because you know that your brothers throughout the world are undergoing the same kind of sufferings. And the God of all grace, who called you to his eternal glory in Christ, after you have suffered a little while, will himself restore you and make you strong, firm and steadfast" (1 Peter 5:8-10).

Daniel and the Demons

The Bible tells of several specific instances where Satan has directly hindered prayers.

In his book, Daniel tells about several miraculous answers to his prayers. For instance: "While I was speaking and . . . making my request to the LORD my God for his holy hill—while I was still in prayer, Gabriel, the man I had seen in the earlier vision, came to me in swift flight . . . and said to me, 'Daniel, I have now come to give you insight and understanding. As soon as you began to pray, an answer was given, which I have come to tell you . . .' " (Daniel 9:20-23).

But not all answers arrived on Daniel's doorstep in swift flight; a few years later, he had a much rougher time getting a response. "I, Daniel, mourned for three weeks. I ate no choice food; no meat or wine touched my lips; and I used no lotions at all until the three weeks were over," he said.

Eventually, while Daniel was standing on the bank of Babylon's Tigris River, an angel again came to him and said, "Do not be afraid, Daniel. Since the first day that you set your mind to gain understanding and to humble yourself before your God, your words were heard, and I have come in response to them. But the prince of the Persian kingdom resisted me twenty-one days. Then Michael, one of the chief princes, came to help me, because I was detained there with the king of Persia. Now I have come to explain . . ." (Daniel 10:2-3, 12-14).

Here we clearly see demons resisting, hindering and delaying the answer to Daniel's prayer. Notice that Daniel played no part in the battle between the angels and demons; his duty was to stay faithful in prayer and leave the timing of the answer to God.

When our prayers are not answered quickly, are demons always the hindrance? Of course not. Sometimes God's own Holy Spirit guides us by hindering us. A prime example of this is found in the missionary journey of Paul, Silas and Timothy: "Paul and his companions traveled throughout the region of Phrygia and Galatia, having been kept by the Holy Spirit from preaching the word in the province of Asia. When they came to the border of Mysia, they tried to enter Bithynia, but the Spirit of Jesus would not allow them to" (Acts 16:6-7).

The context makes it clear that these Christians were praying about where they should travel. They intended to go this place and that, but they were prevented by the Holy Spirit. They continued praying until St. Paul received his "Macedonian vision," telling him to go to Greece.

So . . . how do you know whether it is the Holy Spirit or an angel-fighting demon who is delaying your prayer's answer?

I have no idea.

I'm not sure that we can know until after the event. There is no reason for us to know. Our clear duty is to continue in prayer however long it takes till God's will is plain to us. What practical difference does it make *why* a prayer's answer is delayed, so long as that delay leads us to further prayer?

Job and Satan

Another example of Satan's meddling with a man's prayers appears in the book of Job. Job prayed for his seven sons and three daughters every day. Satan challenged God about the "hedge" of protection around Job. Shortly afterward, a tornado smashed into the house where the children were attending a feast and killed them all instantly.

Job got up, tore his robes, shaved his head, fell to the ground and worshiped the Lord.

Reading the whole book of Job, we see other disasters fall on the poor man's head. "Satan went out from the presence of the LORD and afflicted Job with painful sores from the soles of his feet to the top of his head" (Job 2:7).

Job was in bad shape. He did not understand what was happening to him. But he did as we should do when we don't understand: he continued in the plain duties of the moment, and he continued to pray. In the midst of his pain Job cried:

I know that my Redeemer lives,

and that in the end he will stand upon the earth.

And after my skin has been destroyed,

yet in my flesh I will see God;

I myself will see him

with my own eyes—I, and not another.

How my heart yearns within me! (Job 19:25-27)

In C. S. Lewis's book *The Screwtape Letters,* the demon complains that hell's cause is never more in danger than when a human, no longer desiring but still intending to do God's will, looks round upon a universe from which every trace of God seems to have vanished, and questions why he has been forsaken—but still obeys.

Evil's Victory Overturned
Now demons are subtle, insidious, spoiled, envious, spiteful, cunning and nasty; but they sometimes aren't too bright. They meddle in prayers and other good things, but sometimes their own meddling turns against them.

Think about Satan and Jesus for a bit.

After the first man and woman's fall in the Garden of Eden, God immediately told the snake of the Messiah's coming: the Seed of the Woman would crush the serpent's head even as the serpent bit his heel. (See Genesis 3:15.)

At the birth of Christ, Satan influenced King Herod to murder babies in order to kill the promised King of the Jews. Satan tempted Christ to pray to him in the wilderness. When Jesus exorcised demons, Satan influenced mobs of people to try to stone him or throw him over a cliff. Jesus knew that he would be tortured to death, but continued doing the will of his Father anyhow. Then Satan entered into Judas Iscariot, leading him to betray Jesus.

How Satan must have laughed at the prayers of Jesus in Gethsemane! How pleased he was to see the crown of thorns pressed on the Lord's head. He counted every lash of the whip. He shouted with the mob, "Crucify him! Crucify him!"

And Satan felt glee when he saw Christ nailed down, when he saw Christ die.

All of that evil activity constituted the worm's bite on the Seed of the Woman's heel.

Cover your head, Devil, here comes that heel again!

How do you nail down the Lord of life?

Remember that odd verse in Matthew's Gospel about how when

Christ died, some graves opened and the bodies of saints who slept awoke (Matthew 27:52-53)? I have a mental picture of those entombed bodies: Like dried beans they lie scattered, still and quiet, on the surface of a trampoline. Then somebody climbs a ladder with a cinder block and drops it from ten feet up. Look at those bodies bounce up when our Solid Rock hits the grave!

Who's laughing now, Devil?

Bug off, Worm.

But the best is yet to come. The borrowed tomb of Jesus was a hardhat area for Satan, and he'd left his home.

Not only did Jesus liberate the spirits in prison (whatever that means), but *he arose!*

Job knew it. You and I know it. Paul knew it. But the prince of this age did not know what hit him.

As Paul said: "We speak of God's secret wisdom, a wisdom that has been hidden and that God destined for our glory before time began. None of the rulers of this age understood it, for if they had, they would not have crucified the Lord of glory" (1 Corinthians 2:7-8).

Still, the story gets even better for you and me. Because Christ arose, you and I will rise too!

"Christ has indeed been raised from the dead, the firstfruits of those who have fallen asleep. . . . But each in his own turn: Christ, the firstfruits; then, when he comes, those who belong to him. . . . Death has been swallowed up in victory," Paul says in 1 Corinthians 15 (vv. 20, 23, 54).

Satan has lost the battle, but the evil one still thrashes about in spite, just as a beaten human army might—burning crops and cities, plundering homes and poisoning wells, spoiling lives and blowing up bridges—as he retreats before the Victor.

And this ruined battlefield, this scorched earth, which Satan is pillaging in fury, angry over his defeat by Christ—this is where we live and pray and fight.

But just as Christ arose, our turn is coming. We too will arise. We are going to muster out of this army and go to where the fire burns warm on the hearth, where scrumptious smells waft in from the kitchen, where the good life we have prayed for all our earthly lives awaits us.

We are going Home—where every prayer is fully and unquestionably answered.

— seventeen —

Perfect Prayer

If my prayer

isn't worded just right,

will God answer me?

I N THE TWENTY-FIVE YEARS WE HAVE BEEN MARRIED, MY WIFE has only slapped me once—so far.

She whacked me because of a prayer.

Not one of my prayers, or one of hers. But because of the prayers of three women we'd never seen before and we've never seen since.

I should say right off that Ginny is a charitable woman. On a freezing night I've seen her strip blankets off her own bed and take them to the unheated home of a stranger she'd heard about. But living with me can exasperate the patience of even such a saint.

Here's what happened. That Sunday morning I'd taken my family across town to worship at a service where a friend was the guest speaker. This particular Sunday fell between paydays. *Far* between paydays. In fact, the gas gauge in our car read empty when we left church, and I had only one dollar to buy more gas.

(This was, however, back before the oil crisis, when gas cost 37 cents per gallon.)

Ginny and I were both anxious, worried that we would not even have gas enough to make it to a filling station. Poverty creates tension. But we coasted along on fumes and faith. As we crossed Jacksonville's Main Street Bridge, we saw a wonderful sight below us in the St. Johns River. An antique, three-masted, wooden sailing ship was tied up on the waterfront. We turned off Main Street and stopped to let the children see this magnificent ship.

The ship was named *Unicorn*. Naturally, its figurehead was a unicorn with golden mane, its horn projecting into the waves. Intriguing lattices of taut lines climbed the masts, making a spiderweb of nautical purpose. Seamen had polished the wooden decks and rails to a gleaming finish, punctuated by sparkling brass fittings. One of the men allowed us to board, and our children—except little Eve, who shyly clung to my hand—ran here and there, delighted to be pretend pirates.

My wife minded the other kids on board while Eve and I wandered back down to the wharf to get a closer look at the golden unicorn figurehead.

As we walked down the gangplank, I noticed three women standing by a rail on the cement seawall. Two had white hair and wore white blouses and billowing black skirts; the third was much younger.

At first I thought the trio were enjoying an after-church outing to feed sea gulls. The older women had a black coffee-table-size Bible lying open on top of the rail; its fluttering pages were anchored open by a loaf of bread.

Then I saw that the younger woman was crying.

The older women would huddle together awhile, hugging the younger one. Then one would wing a slice of bread out over the river. Ever-hungry gulls swooped for the bread, but the women ignored them. After each slice was tossed, all three would wave their hands in the air for a bit, then go back into their huddle.

I was intrigued. What in the world were these people doing? Eve and I wandered closer and closer to them, curious about their bizarre behavior. I couldn't figure it out. The only way to find out was to ask. So I did.

"We is a-praying," one of the women answered. "This here child got a terrible need, and the Book say if you got such a need, then you go to the river and cast your bread on the water, and God will increase it to meet you's need."

I realized that none of these dear saints knew how to read; the King James Bible verse she was referring to is Ecclesiastes 11:1, which says, "Cast thy bread upon the waters: for thou shalt find it after many days." Many Bible scholars think the obscure Hebrew words in this verse have something to do with the import-export business. They translate it to mean "Send your grain across the seas, and in time you will get a return." Or "Invest your money in foreign trade, and one of these days you will make a profit."

Now God only knows what that verse really means. But one thing is certain: no Bible scholar anywhere thinks it means that if you toss a Wonder Bread Frisbee in the St. Johns River, God will send you cash.

But these three simple women could not read the opinions of eminent Bible scholars. They just felt that if they called on the name of the Lord and obeyed him as best they knew how, then he would not let them down.

Okay. Okay. I know I did wrong. I know I am guilty of promoting an ignorant superstition. I know the Bible is not a rabbit's foot . . .

But confronted by the simple, childlike faith of these women who were praying the best they knew how, I could not—I just could not—walk away. Especially knowing that I had that dollar for gas in my pocket. I just couldn't do it.

I gave the oldest woman the dollar and apologized for not having more.

She hugged her friends, and they jumped up and down and cried,

"Thank you, Jesus! Thank you, Jesus."

She said, "See here, girl, I done tolt you that God answers prayer, and he's just getting started!"

They went back to casting their bread on the St. Johns and praying, while Eve and I joined the rest of the family back at the car. By now I was doing some praying of my own: "Dear Jesus, I sure hope the gas gauge is wrong. Let me have gas enough to at least make it home."

Well, we'd driven a few blocks when Eve, now a refined young woman who enters beauty pageants but then a five-year-old snitch, piped up from the back seat, "Daddy, why did you give those ladies that money?"

"John! You didn't!" my poor shocked wife cried. "You couldn't have!"

"Now, honey—" I began.

"Don't you honey me," she said—and popped me a good one.

Who could blame her? I deserved it.

Anyhow, we did have gas enough to make it home—barely. Payday finally did arrive. No harm done, unless it was the harm I did in encouraging those women to treat a Bible verse like a magic charm.

Oddly enough, to this day whenever my own cash runs low, I remember those three women at the river, and as I pray for me, I pray for them again.

And I'm thankful for them too. They taught me that prayer does not have to be perfect.

We can—and probably do more often than we realize—pray in ignorance. We can garble the words and misunderstand the Scripture. We can read prayers from a book, or we can just sob inarticulately.

Nevertheless, in spite of all the confusion I feel regarding prayer, in spite of my questioning why my prayers sometimes do not seem to be answered, in spite of all my doubts, I believe—I am firmly convinced—that if we sincerely call to Jesus for help, if we obey him to the best of our understanding, he will hear . . . and he will answer.

This is what the LORD says, he who made the earth, the LORD who formed it and established it—the LORD is his name: "Call to me and I will answer you and tell you great and unsearchable things you do not know." (Jeremiah 33:2-3)

Bibliography

Augustine of Hippo. *The Confessions of St. Augustine.* Trans. E. M. Blaiklock. Nashville: Thomas Nelson, 1983.

Bailey, Faith Cox. *George Mueller.* Chicago: Moody Press, 1958.

Barbet, Pierre. *A Doctor at Calvary: The Passion of Our Lord Jesus Christ As Described by a Surgeon.* New York: Image Books, 1963.

Bishop, Jim. *The Day Christ Died.* New York: Harper & Brothers, 1957.

The Book of Common Prayer. New York: James Pott, 1929.

Browne, Thomas. *Religio Medici.* New York: Appleton-Century-Crofts, 1966.

Cowart, John W. *People Whose Faith Got Them into Trouble.* Downers Grove, Ill.: InterVarsity Press, 1990.

_____. "Prayer Works." *Florida Times-Union,* May 5, 1984.

Edwards, Jonathan. *Basic Writings.* New York: New American Library, 1966.

1862—Forever Free. Vol. 3 of *The Civil War* (videotape).

Farrar, F. W. *The Early Days of Christianity.* New York: Funk & Wagnalls, 1883.

Fénelon, François. *Christian Perfection.* New York: Harper & Brothers, 1947.

_____. *Spiritual Letters.* Auburn, Maine: Christian Books Publishing, 1982.

Finegan, Jack. *Light from the Ancient Past.* Princeton, N.J.: Princeton University Press, 1946.

Foreman, Dale. *Crucify Him: A Lawyer Looks at the Trial of Jesus.* Grand Rapids, Mich.: Zondervan, 1990.

Gordon, S. D. *Quiet Talks on Prayer.* New York: Fleming H. Revell, 1904.

Graham, Billy. *Billy Graham Answers Your Questions.* Minneapolis: World Wide Publications, n.d.

Hallesby, O. *Prayer.* Minneapolis: Augsburg, 1931.

Hyman, Ann. "Exorcising Ghosts Is a Group Effort." *Florida Times-Union,* September 25, 1991.

The Kneeling Christian. Grand Rapids, Mich.: Zondervan, 1945.

Landers, Peggy. "An Interview with Terry Waite." Knight-Ridder Newspapers, typescript.

Laubach, Frank C. *Prayer: The Mightiest Force in the World.* Old Tappan, N.J.: Fleming H. Revell, 1946.

Law, William. *A Serious Call to a Devout and Holy Life.* London: I. M. Dent & Sons, 1906.

Lawrence, Brother. *The Practice of the Presence of God.* Old Tappan, N.J.: Fleming H. Revell, 1958.

Lewis, C. S. *God in the Dock.* Grand Rapids, Mich.: Eerdmans, 1970.

Loehr, Franklin. *The Power of Prayer on Plants.* New York: Doubleday, 1959.

Miller, Basil. *Praying Hyde: A Man of Prayer.* Grand Rapids, Mich.: Zondervan, 1943.

Moltmann, Jürgen. *The Crucified God.* San Francisco: Harper & Row, 1974.

Murray, Andrew. *The Prayer Life.* Chicago: Moody Press, n.d.

_____. *The True Vine.* Chicago: Moody Press, n.d.

Pearce, Roy Harvey, ed. *Colonial American Writing.* New York: Holt, Rinehart and Winston, 1950.

Plato. *Great Dialogues of Plato.* Ed. Eric H. Warmington. Trans.

W. H. D. Rouse. New York: New American Library, 1956.

Smedes, Lewis B. *A Pretty Good Person.* San Francisco: Harper, 1990.

Spurgeon, C. H. *Evening by Evening.* Grand Rapids, Mich.: Baker Book House, 1975.

Strong, James. *Strong's Exhaustive Concordance to the Holy Bible.* Nashville: Crusade Bible Publishers, n.d.

Swanson, Kenneth. *Uncommon Prayer: Approaching Intimacy with God.* New York: Ballantine, 1987.

Taylor, Jeremy. *The Rule and Exercises of Holy Living.* New York: Harper & Row, 1970.

"This Primate of a Different Denomination." *Florida Times-Union,* March 2, 1992.

Thomas à Kempis. *Of the Imitation of Christ.* New York: Oxford University Press, 1917.

Tozer, A. W. *The Knowledge of the Holy.* San Francisco: Harper & Row, 1961.

Vernon, Edward, trans. *The Gospel of St. Mark: A New Translation in Simple English from the Nestle Greek Text.* New York: Prentice-Hall, 1952.